TWO LIVES

TWO LIVES

REEVE LINDBERGH

Two Lives

Brigantine Media/Voyage
211 North Avenue
St. Johnsbury, Vermont 05819
Phone: 802-751-8802
Fax: 802-751-8804
E-mail: neil@brigantinemedia.com
Website: www.brigantinemedia.com

Brigantine Media/Voyage publications are available through most
booksellers.
They can also be ordered directly from the publisher.
Phone: 802-751-8802 | Fax: 802-751-8804
www.brigantinemedia.com
ISBN 978-1-9384067-0-6

For Nat, and for the family

CONTENTS

TWO LIVES

I often think I live two lives, one in the foreground and the other in the background, each life taking its turn. I have a real or normal life in the country, where my husband and I live on an old farm at the end of a dirt road. We wear comfortable clothes, write books, raise sheep and chickens, are active in community life, and welcome our children and grandchildren whenever they come to visit.

There is also an entirely different "Lindbergh" life, which requires putting on somewhat less comfortable clothes and traveling to places away from the farm, where I attend meetings and give talks and where there are no chickens except for the kind on the menu followed by words like "cordon bleu" and "a la king" and "Kiev." In this second life, I stand up in front of groups of people and talk a little about the books I have written for children and adults, and a lot about the lives of my late parents, Charles A. and Anne Morrow Lindbergh.

I have spoken about my parents on college campuses and Air Force bases, in museums and libraries and schools, to children and to adults around the country for many decades. When I have finished with the meetings or the talks, I come home to Vermont, change clothes, and emerge from the limbo of travel and from my Lindbergh life. I settle down with my husband, the dogs, the sheep, and the chickens, immersing myself in farm and community until the next time, when I put on my other wardrobe again and out I go.

Maybe it is a strange way to live, coming and going and switching focus completely between one life and the other, moving from the present to the past—not even my own past, but my parents'—and back again. Still, I've done this for so long that it feels like just another part of my routine, like going to the farmers market or taking one of the dogs to the vet. One of the chief differences is that in my Lindbergh life there are different questions to answer. Instead of "How long has she been limping?" or "Do you want a bag for these?" it's "What is your favorite memory of your father?" or "Did your mother teach you to write?" or "What can you tell us about the kidnapping?" or "Did your father really have other families?"

These questions are now so familiar that they don't trouble me much, though I can remember when some of them did. I first began to live two lives not long after my father's death in 1974. Before that, my father and my mother spoke for themselves, if they chose to speak at all. Most of their communication with the world was done in writing. Between the two of them, they published more than twenty books about their lives and reflections over the years.

My father rarely spoke in public during my childhood in the late 1940s and the 1950s, though he had done so before I was born. He made speeches on behalf of the future of aviation after his 1927 flight from New York to Paris, when he was in his mid-twenties, and he spoke out against America's entrance into the Second World War as part of the now controversial Isolationist movement when he was in his late thirties. Toward the end of his life, when he was in his sixties and I in my late teens and twenties, he began to speak out again. This time, he talked about his growing concern for the environment worldwide and his conviction that we must achieve "balance" between the rapid development of technology and the preservation of nature. He spoke in the House chamber in Juneau, Alaska, in support of a bill that State Senator Lowell Thomas Jr. was proposing for the protection of arctic wolves. He spoke to a radio audience in the Philippines on behalf of what was then called the "monkey-eating eagle" but is now known as the Philippine eagle and recently has been proclaimed the national bird of the Philippines.

He gave a speech in 1973 at his boyhood home in Little Falls, Minnesota, in which he reminisced about summers sleeping on the screened porch of that home not far from the banks of the upper Mississippi River. He told the audience how very pleased he was that his boyhood home was now a national park, named in honor of his own father, C. A. Lindbergh. My father had come to believe that the establishment of parks and wilderness areas was a far greater sign of human progress than anything technology had achieved.

I wasn't present for the speech itself, but have read it in print and have seen and heard him deliver it on film. He died in Maui, Hawaii, in 1974, only a year later. I like to think of my father returning to his childhood home as he neared the end of his life, remembering his Minnesota childhood and telling a local audience what he had come to care about more than anything else in the course of a full and adventurous life.

I knew him best during this time, his "conservation years," when his focus was absolute, as it had always been absolute, on whatever project or passion engaged him. He talked fervidly about his efforts to save the monkey-eating eagle in the Philippines, the blue whale in Japan, and the wildlife of East Africa. He was so electrically energetic that even when he was away, his influence remained and reverberated throughout the house.

My mother was a different story entirely. During my childhood, our father was present even in his absence: his energy, his rules, his discipline lingering in the house as did the woodsy outdoor scent of his winter jacket in the hall closet. Our mother, however, had the ability to be absent within her presence. She was completely with me, especially when I needed her. She always listened to my stories, always took my physical and emotional complaints seriously, and did not disappear into the world for weeks or months, the way our father did. Still, she could go deeply into herself when I was sitting right there next to her. Her eyes would look off and away through the window over the mudflats and marsh grasses of Long Island Sound, one hand fingering a brooch at her neck. I remember it as a cameo in a silver frame, with a bouquet of flowers against a black background, all fashioned of tiny, colorful, semi-precious stones. I knew that she was still there with me, but that she was also somewhere else.

It was my mother who provided the steady, gentle background of my earliest days, in her knee-length floral-print dresses and her dark, curly hair held up and back at the sides in what I later learned was a common 1940s style, a kind of upward roll on both sides of the face with another roll over the forehead. My mother's coiffure was looser, curlier, and much less Hollywood-glamorous than Betty Grable's or Ava Gardner's, but her hairdresser may have been trying for the same effect.

My mother spoke in public only occasionally, when invited to do so by an organization with which she was associated, or by family members and friends. She liked to read aloud a piece she had carefully written ahead of time for the event, which might be an alumnae program at Smith College, her granddaughter's graduation at Middlebury, or a talk given to members of the Cosmopolitan Club in New York City.

When my parents spoke in public, there was rarely a question period after the talk. My father disliked being questioned to begin with, and had been uncomfortable with what he called "the press" ever since his flight to Paris in 1927. My mother said that once when they were about to embark on one of their early survey flights together, a reporter begged her husband to reveal, at least, which direction they were planning to take on this journey. My father responded solemnly, "Up."

Over the course of his lifetime, my father became increasingly adept at disappearances. Even in Little Falls in 1973, I cannot believe he would have been available to the crowd the way other speakers are after giving a talk. I imagine him slipping away before anybody in the audience could approach him, safe in the protective custody of the Minnesota Historical Society staff.

My mother, too, always had protectors for her speeches—I was often one of them—in the form of companions who took her away to find a cup of tea or a place to rest following her presentation. It was characteristic of both of my parents to be quite open to the world in their spoken or written words, but much less willing to share themselves in person.

But unlike my parents, I always expect to have questions from the audience after I give a talk. I often enjoy the "questions" part of the program best, in fact, because it feels like a conversation. I am relieved of the burden of doing all the talking, and I don't have to listen to myself, which can become tedious if you offer more or less the same presentation to different groups, as I do when I talk about my family.

Sometimes a tactful moderator asks whether there are things I'd prefer not to talk about, questions that might be painful or difficult for me to answer. I always say that I will answer any question I'm asked to the best of my ability, though there may be questions to which I don't know the answer. A wonderful thing that has happened to me after many years of speaking in public is that I have completely lost my fear of answering questions, and have gained the great freedom of simply telling the truth, as far as I know it.

I'm pretty sure that I'm not alone in living two lives. I think most people do this to some degree. When a person gets up in the morning and goes to school or to work, he or she leaves an "at home" self behind. Salespeople have salesmanship selves, office workers have at-the-office selves, any teacher, whether in kindergarten or in college, has developed a teaching self. A teacher needs to be "on" in a certain way, just as an actor is "on" for the theater, film, or television. When the school day is over or the cameras have stopped rolling or the stage lights have dimmed, then you can be "off"—just yourself again.

The difference for me is that I'm never entirely "off." Even when I think that I am completely free of it, Lindbergh life seeps into my everyday existence at the most unexpected moments. Then I find I have to move from a kind of low-key, daily consciousness concerned with things like laundry, shopping, working in my garden, and asking people to bake pies for the library bake sale to another way of thinking entirely, a state of mind blended from instinct, training, and long experience. This is the way I confront my family's past.

Hardly a day goes by, and never as much as a week, that I do not receive correspondence related to my father's aviation career, my parents' personal lives, my mother's and father's historical archives and literary legacies. One day, for instance, I received two requests: one from a group hoping to name their new in-flight magazine *Lindbergh*, "because we believe that Charles Lindbergh personified the pioneering spirit, intelligence, and elegance the magazine will strive for," and another for an interview to discuss my father's 1927 flight to Paris.

I was able to respond to both requests easily. In the first case, the family still follows my parents' policy not to use their names or likenesses for commercial purposes; in the second, I'd be glad to talk to the historian about my father's flight to Paris, but since it occurred eighteen years before I was born, everything I know about it came from his books. My father rarely even mentioned that flight to me. If I asked him about it he invariably responded, "Read my book." Eventually, I did. I read all his books and all my mother's, and I keep on reading them because I need to.

Most of the ongoing Lindbergh literary responsibilities came to me after my parents died because I have worked with editors and publishers in my own writing life for more than thirty years. I have also dealt with my mother's and father's letters, manuscripts, and archives since the death of first one and then both of my parents. Even though my father has been dead for more than forty years and my mother for fifteen, their written words continue to reverberate in my consciousness, and their lives still trail long tendrils across mine.

Hundreds of other people, even now, are just as interested in my family as I am. Some of them are much more interested than I am. Those Lindbergh researchers and biographers and scholars have been so helpful in supplying dates and times, and verifying the accuracy of my own memories: How old was I when my father and I had a forced landing together? What year was it when my mother became the first licensed female glider pilot in the United States?

I used to pester A. Scott Berg with questions like these when he was writing *Lindbergh*, his Pulitzer-prize winning biography of my father. During this time, I was writing my first memoir, *Under a Wing*, about growing up in my family. Scott also asked me questions, but he did so very discreetly and politely. Once, probably because I had expressed astonishment at hearing how many boxes of material he proposed to go through in the Lindbergh collection at the Sterling Library at Yale (seven hundred, I think he said), he almost complained to me about some of the material he had discovered, items that had been saved by my parents and sent to the university to be kept there in perpetuity. Was it really necessary, he wondered, to save carbon copies of the handwritten notes to our teachers excusing us from school for dental appointments? Small squares of blotting paper, probably made by cutting one of my mother's large desk blotters into smaller pieces, with each square covered with the indecipherable reverse-blottings of words from letters or diaries or grocery lists? Did I have any ideas about all this?

I told him, because I could not resist, that at our house during my high school years there were always two cardboard boxes sitting at the top of the stairs to the basement. Next to the basement was the attached garage where my father kept the station wagon he used for local errands. He also drove this car to New Haven when he carried documents to the Yale archives. One box at the top of the basement stairs was labeled "YALE," for the station wagon. The other was labeled "DUMP." Could the labels, or the boxes, have been switched?

If he had not been so well brought up, I think Scott would have hung up on me. It sometimes seemed to me that my father and mother either did not know how to separate archival material from what should be considered garbage, or did not have time to sort the material carefully before bringing the next load of boxes to Yale. My father was usually so meticulous in his habits that I was surprised at some of the things we found when I visited the library a few years ago with my brother Land, our niece Kristina, and our friend and assistant Carol Hyman. We were there to help the archivists make sense of some of the more questionable items in the Lindbergh collection: folders full of brochures for summer camps that we children had attended over the years, along with brochures for summer camps that we did *not* attend; my brother Land's kindergarten paintings, about which he expressed the opinion that our mother had always had a feeling for fine art; pale slips of mimeographed notices announcing PTA meetings and teachers' conferences at our schools.

None of the archivists had felt they could discard this material without permission from the family. Poor archivists! We weeded out a good deal of it, though I'm not sure we dared to discard the kindergarten paintings.

Despite my occasional complaints I am still fascinated by the celebrity that surrounded my parents for most of their lives, no matter how hard they tried to escape it. I have an impulse to explore this phenomenon further, and another, even stronger one that wants to do exactly the opposite: fight against it, wrestle it down to human scale by bringing into the picture everything familiar and genuine that I know about my parents—my father's toothbrush, his comb and the handkerchief in his pocket, the bright Mexican ribbons my mother wore in her hair, her underwear and stockings dripping over the shower curtain railing in the bathroom to dry, the horse chestnuts she kept in her coat pockets, shining deep mahogany from the invisible rubbing of her thumb.

It seems to me now that fame, like disease or war, is the enemy of normal human life. It certainly was for my parents, especially during their first years together. I was ignorant in my childhood of something that became very clear to me later. My parents had no wish to live in the past for many reasons, but the greatest of those must have been that their early adventures were followed by terrible tragedy; the extraordinary fame of the 1920s and early 1930s had directly contributed to the kidnapping death of their first child, Charles, in 1932. After that horror, their lives changed completely. They left America, living for a time in England and in France with my older brothers, and they shunned all forms of publicity for the greater part of their lives. Having been robbed of normalcy in a terrible way early on, they understood it for the treasure that it is, and tried their best to offer this treasure to their children as we grew up. How little I appreciated their efforts.

I hated having to memorize a false surname when we were on vacation—"Scott," Spencer"—names close enough to our family to remember, though I always forgot which one we were using at the time. How outraged I was if my father made us get up and leave a restaurant because one of the waiters asked for his autograph. How embarrassed I felt!

The amount of attention that comes to me because of my parents' fame is a tiny fraction of what they faced every day during the time I was growing up. Still, when the past comes calling, whatever my circumstances may be at the time, I immediately snap into Lindbergh mode. I can't help it.

Recently, my husband was diagnosed with bladder cancer. A tumor discovered during a checkup was surgically removed the same day, a second surgery followed within the month, and we were plunged into what I think of as Cancer Limbo: the time when a family knows the disease has struck but has yet to find out what the prognosis will be.

I was thinking about my husband's health all the time, driving back and forth with him to a hospital an hour away, feeding the sheep and chickens while trying to keep our spirits up and the two of us fed. He is the cook in the family, as well as the gardener, and he's much better than I am in both areas, so for me, it was a matter of trying to keep the standards up. Some of our children arrived to help out, and communications within the family circle were constant and intense.

At some time during this period, a friend received an e-mail message from a woman who was aware that he knew me, and my friend sent the message my way as she had requested. The woman's late father had always thought he might be the "Missing Lindbergh Baby." His daughter attached several photographs to the email to show how much this man had, or believed he had, looked like my father. I was unable to see the resemblance, though he was certainly a good-looking man and his daughter clearly loved him and respected his belief that he was related to my family.

It might have seemed odd to move into Lindbergh mode, that week of all weeks, but I did it instinctively.

The only answer I had for this woman was one that would disappoint her. It's the same answer I have given over and over, for many decades, to people who believe that they or one of their relatives is really my "long-lost brother," the "Missing Lindbergh Baby": There is no "Missing Lindbergh Baby." I never had a "long-lost brother." There was a dead child, my brother Charles, whose body was found a number of weeks after he had been kidnapped from his home in Hopewell, New Jersey, in 1932. He was wearing his own clothes, with his own teeth in his head, and he was identified by his doctor as well as his father, my father. Still, for some reason, some people have made a mystery of this tragedy for all the eighty-odd intervening years.

I will never understand how the stark fact of that child's death, a horrific injustice cutting short a life that had barely begun, has been lost again and again in so many bewildering apocryphal stories: the myth of the "Missing Lindbergh Baby," the conspiracy theories implicating either my father, one of my aunts, other household members, or completely unassociated individuals whose names were in the news at the same time, including Al Capone.

The truth is that a very young child died during the course of a botched kidnapping, and his body was later found in the woods near his home. It was terrible, heartbreaking, and I don't think that my parents ever really got over it. It affected their individual lives and the life of their marriage forever. The fact and manner of my brother's death still shocks me every time something reminds me of it, even though he died more than eight decades ago and before I was born, and even if I am in the midst of a present-day family crisis.

I can sympathize with someone else's difficult family story, and I can be sorry that another family history has linked itself with my family's long-ago loss, but to feel that sympathy and to be sorry about another family is as far away as I can move from the child who died, my parent's first son, my brother. He, the real child, is the heart of the case and remains close to my heart too, though I never knew him.

During our time of medical intensity and Cancer Limbo, we received many messages and phone calls from our loved ones: our children, my brothers, cousins, nieces, and nephews, my husband's family and friends. I also got a call from a beloved half-brother in Europe. I was unaware of this man's existence until 2003, when I traveled overseas to meet my half-brothers and half-sisters, the children of my father's relationships with three women he had come to know after the Second World War. These were women who knew each other: two of them were sisters, the other was their friend. Our father had visited them all regularly and had provided for them financially.

I first found out about them through a letter from a half-brother whose mother was still living. He felt very strongly, as she did, that the situation should remain private. I did not understand what he meant by "the situation" until I read the news reports generated by another of these European families. Their mother had died the same year my mother did, and her children saw no reason not to reveal themselves. The remaining two of the three families followed their mothers' wishes and tried to remain out of the public eye. Though they did make friendly contact with our own family, they did so in a very private way.

I traveled to Europe and met all of my half-siblings in the summer of 2003. I visited the home of one of the very discreet half-brothers during that summer, and we talked a lot during my visit. We took long walks together, speaking in English or in French, whichever was easiest at the moment. His English is better than my French, so we usually speak English during the telephone calls we have shared regularly over the years since that summer.

I have come to know and love this man since our meeting, and I am glad that we can speak together often. In the midst of our Cancer

Limbo, with doctors' appointments and medical procedures and worry all the time, he called me from Europe as usual, and I told him the medical situation. He responded with characteristically thoughtful concern, and during the following weeks he sent several notes and postcards, which I carried with me and read over while waiting for my husband's second surgical procedure to be completed.

While I was re-reading my half-brother's postcards and thinking about his warmhearted concern for me and my family, I understood something simple, yet stunning. It had little to do with jumping in and out of Lindbergh mode, or with celebrity, or even with history. Whatever the trouble, sorrows or confusion there may be in either or both of my lives, whatever is disturbing, confusing, or bizarre about being a Lindbergh, it has brought me unexpected comfort to know that I do have a long-lost brother, after all.

CHICKEN YOGA, ROOSTER SOUP

We have kept chickens for over forty years. Not the same chickens for the whole time, though it sometimes seems that way. There is always a Bad Hen, ill-tempered and ready to strike—and strike hard—should you try to sneak a hand beneath her feathery breast and extract an egg from the nesting box where she huddles so sweetly. There's always at least one swaggering Macho Rooster, there are always a few ditsy pullets hiding in the barn rafters when it's time to come in at night, and there's always one gawky half-grown chick that turns out to be the prettiest hen in the whole flock.

That's the way it is with chickens. To everything there is a season, and in every season—in my life, at least—there are chickens. We've raised chickens for so long that we've seen it all, or maybe I should say we've seen most of it. There may be some surprises yet in store because, again, that's the way it is with chickens. Surprising.

Some of the surprises have to do with eggs. Eggs are the reason we have chickens in the first place. I don't care what anybody says, store-bought eggs don't taste as good as fresh-laid farm eggs, ever. Sometimes we get bountiful quantities, clutches of rich brown or bright white or even blue-ish-green eggs—those are from the Araucanas—sitting quietly in the nesting boxes for me to gather and place in the egg-collecting basket I carry with me for this purpose. Sometimes the eggs are warm and clean, just waiting for my hand to curl around them, pick them up and take them away. Sometimes they are lightly speckled and blotched with brown spots, which may or may not be part of the egg's natural coloring. If not, they need cleaning off with a wet paper towel before they are put away in the egg cartons in the refrigerator, but that's easy enough.

But there are other times. The hens go on strike for extended periods. They just don't lay any eggs at all. Some people tell me this happens because our hens are old, and some of them certainly are. Other people tell me that our hens don't get enough light in the winter months, and that we should keep a light bulb burning in the barn. We would do this except that Nat, the spoilsport, doesn't want to burn the barn down. There are also people who advise us to feed the hens something other than just plain "Layer Pellets" from the grain store. ("*Lay-Eggs-Frequently* Pellets"?)

I tend to believe all the advice I'm given, so I start to think about doing something different with the hens, but just when I'm about to do it, they all start laying eggs again. They lay eggs in the nesting boxes and they lay eggs on the chicken room floor and they lay eggs in hidden places in the hayloft. That's a real problem. When you're stacking hay bales in the barn in July, the last thing you want to have underfoot is a rotten egg from last year, unless it's a screeching hen who thinks you're a home invader.

Maybe there would be fewer surprises if the chickens were more closely confined, but what fun is that? The whole point of getting eggs from free-range chickens is that the chickens range free. They go forth in the morning from the chicken coop (or chicken room, in our case) as soon as the door has been opened, and they scratch for feed, gravel, and insects all over the driveway and the yard and the fields and the flower garden. In the evening, they come trooping back into the open chicken room door again, and spend the night up on their roosts, softly sleeping.

Unless they don't. There are outliers in any flock, which means out-layers and out-roosters. Their souls are independent, their roosting locations unpredictable—in the hayloft, in the upper eaves of the barn, snuggled up next to a nest of outraged barn swallows—and their eggs are everywhere. It's a miracle if I find them before the dogs do.

As the days grow shorter and the nights get longer, the wanderers often straggle in toward the warmth of their fellows in the chicken room toward evening, but there are always holdouts. At this writing—between Thanksgiving and Christmas—there is still one freedom-loving bantam hen with two adolescent chicks, avoiding the inevitable. I don't know where this little family actually spends the night, but every morning when I go out to the barn, bringing food and water for the rest of the flock, these three rush up to me with double-quick chicken steps, picking up their feathered skirts as they go, even though one of the two chicks is definitely planning to be a rooster when he grows up, judging by the size of his comb and by the way he treats his sister.

I should catch this trio and put them into the chicken room with the rest of the hens and our two adult roosters. Sooner or later it will be too cold for chickens to be outside at all, and there are wandering foxes and raccoons abroad on winter nights too. Not only that, but if one of the out-layer hens does lay an egg, I'll never find it.

It has also occurred to me that putting these new, semi-wild chickens (feral chickens?) into the chicken room might increase production all around. It has been known to happen. In fact, it works every time we chicken-sit for a couple we know, Tom and HyonBy Wales (pronounced "Yon Bee") who have half a dozen very beautiful, sleek-looking hens, but prefer not to travel with them. This well-fed flock lives in town, on Summer Street, and Tom regularly brings one of his hens to a yoga class that is held once a week in a large, sun-filled upstairs room of their house. It is a very small yoga class, only four people, the teacher, and sometimes the hen. The hen, a white Leghorn, struts about with great dignity among the yoga mats before we begin. She looks as if she's either going to lay an egg or do an asana, but would not dream of depositing anything that would need to be cleaned up. Tom claims that the hen comes to visit us before the class in order to provide inspiration, and he may be right.

This hen and her sisters definitely inspire our chickens when they come—on vacation, sort of—to our farm. We call these beauties the

Princesses of Wales. They arrive in a big cardboard box in the back of Tom's car, and when he puts them down gently, one by one, in our chicken room, our flock goes wild. They've never seen anything like this. "Uptown Girls," Tom said once, proudly. I was very worried the first time they came to visit us, about the influences they'd come under down here at the end of the dirt road, but he said that they'd been at the convent school for too long and needed some real world experience. They most certainly got it.

Roosters are not known for restraint, especially where hens are concerned. They are noisily, brutally, and insatiably amorous, chasing the females and biting them fiercely on the back of the neck as they take their pleasure. This can be so appalling to observe inside the chicken room that I stamp my feet and make noise as I approach with my egg basket, hoping to shock them into good behavior before I, the farm mother, enter the scene.

I warned Tom and HyonBy about this, because they don't have any roosters themselves, living as they do within the town limits where roosters are not permitted. Still, Tom decided that his hens could handle the situation, and as it turned out, he was right. He came back to get the Princesses at the end of their ten days with our chickens, and afterwards he said his girls didn't seem any the worse for wear. If he looked closely they maybe looked a little . . . disheveled, but that was all.

A week later he told me that the one thing he'd noticed about his hens after bringing them home was that they seemed a bit depressed. *It's been a whole week since we were together, and he hasn't called, he hasn't written . . .*

The astonishing thing for us, here on the farm, was that the mere presence of the Princesses galvanized our own chickens, and greatly increased egg production by our hens. Where there had been a pathetic dribble, one or two eggs every other day, now there was a steady flow: three, then five, finally as many as six or more warm ovoid treasures in the nesting boxes, every single morning when I came in to feed and water the flock. To be sure, some of these were Princess eggs, big and brown and beautifully formed, as befits a royal bloodline. The others, however, were little bantam eggs and blue-green Araucana eggs and many others that bore the unmistakable signs of our mongrelized and motley brood.

It was a bonanza. We finally were able to fill up a few of the empty egg boxes given to us by generous friends and neighbors. We could give away a dozen eggs to visiting friends when they returned to the city after a weekend here. They bore them off with the same joy that accompanies a gift of maple syrup. "Farm fresh eggs! They taste so much better than store-bought! Ooh! Some of these are *green!*"

Alas, it was a short-lived phenomenon. At about the time the Wales Princesses were moping back at their own home, our hens were on strike again. I don't know whether the problem was the absence of the Princesses as inspiration, or the brutally renewed attentions of the roosters, but suddenly we had no eggs in the nesting boxes at all: no brown ones, no white ones, no blue-ish-green ones, nothing. Day after disappointing day, the egg basket came back from the barn with me as empty as it was when I left the kitchen. The hens were sulkily, self-protectively unproductive, and the roosters were in vicious moods. It wasn't much fun. We began to look at this flock with predatory eyes and growling stomachs. We began to think like the carnivores we are. Eggs are all very well when you can get them, but if you can't get them you think of chicken cacciatore, chicken Kiev, coq au vin and its peasant translation: rooster soup.

I actually like live roosters, up to a point. They are very handsome, and I enjoy all that "cock-a-doodle-doo"-ing, though I've never had a rooster who could tell the time. They don't crow at dawn, whatever you may have learned as a child. They crow all day long, and at the slightest provocation. They crow when the dog barks and when the UPS man drives into the yard. They crow if I open the top of the barrel where the grain is stored, and they crow when Nat feeds the sheep. They crow as soon as I enter the chicken room and they crow when I go out again. They crow because they can, and because they like doing it.

Roosters are also swaggerers and strutters, which is foolish of them, because of the hawks. We had an incident here last summer, an event that Nat still refers to as The Case of the Amazing Exploding Rooster, when a young and gorgeous rooster strutted his stuff and crowed his cock-a-doodle-doo in the driveway for half a day, exuberantly, and then exploded, leaving two or three feathers drifting near the ground and one wild hawk wheeling in the sky above. It happened so fast that it almost didn't seem to have happened at all. What a way to go!

But sometimes there are just too many roosters. Baby chicks grow up quickly, some of them turn out be roosters, and unless you do something about this, the rooster population gets drastically out of hand and the hens suffer in extreme and unjustifiable ways. What's the solution? For us, it's rooster soup.

When I say "us," I mean Nat and Tom, who kill the roosters, and Nat and HyonBy, who cook them. This is how it happened one day not too long ago.

It was a long, cold afternoon on the farm. The two men went back and forth from the barn to the kitchen, where I hovered, waiting around in case I could be helpful, while hoping that Nat and Tom didn't need me. They didn't, because they knew exactly what to do, and my job was to listen to my husband tell me about it afterwards.

"I wring their necks," Nat said. "Then I chop off their heads so they bleed out." He went on to explain that there were other ways to do this job. In Vietnam, where he served as a platoon leader many years ago, farmers would cradle the doomed chicken in their arms, stroke it gently until it was almost asleep, then very quickly slit its throat. He made the process sound almost pleasant. It reminded me of the way the Bosnians who buy sheep from us manage the slaughter of the animals. They come to the farm and kill the selected animal on site, after Nat has separated it from the rest of the flock. The Bosnians handle the chosen victim as gently as possible up to its very last moment of life, on the theory that if an animal has died in terror its meat will be unpleasantly tough.

I am glad to have the Bosnians, whom I know and like, come to kill the sheep right on the farm. In past years, I've hated watching the animals we'd raised go off, baa-ing in protest, in the commercial meat truck. It is true that all of the sheep are very skittish on the day when the Bosnians arrive, and I can certainly understand why. Slaughter on the farm, though I have little or nothing to do with it, is always difficult for me. When Nat is wringing the necks of roosters, I find myself wringing my hands and thinking about becoming a vegetarian. The trouble is, I don't like tofu. (And yes, I have tried it, many times and many ways.) The reason may be that when an adventurous young vegetarian friend prepared a tofu-laden meal for us all years ago, my children were unimpressed and called it "Toad Food." I've been told that vegetarian fare includes a great variety of delicious foods and that tofu never has to be on the menu at all, and I am sure that this is true, but I think I've spent too many years as a carnivore now to give up eating meat. And besides that, Nat makes a truly delicious rooster soup.

This is *bantam* rooster soup. Our roosters are relatively small. Therefore it can be made in a large pot or soup kettle, but does not require the kind of huge container people use for cooking lobsters. Nat plucks and cleans the rooster—no guts, no feathers—puts the rooster in the pot, and then covers it with water to about twice its depth. Then he boils the thing forever—six hours or so—with a bay leaf and some peppercorns, and then he takes it out of the pot again. He puts vegetables in the broth—chopped celery and onions, and carrots and leeks, and lets them all cook together while he's picking the meat, now tender, from the well-boiled bird. Finally, the pieces of meat go back in the pot again, with some rice or noodles and some diced tomatoes, which are probably from a can, since rooster-soup season is never, ever, the middle of the summer. At last, he adds thyme and soy sauce and balsamic vinegar and *nuoc mam*, which is a kind of fish sauce, and everything cooks a little longer. And then, if we're lucky, it's time to have dinner, and if we're even luckier, I've been thinking ahead and there's fresh-baked bread to go with the meal. Homemade bread and rooster soup: there's nothing more delicious on a cold winter evening.

I had come to think that the main reason for roosters, beyond their role in terrorizing hens and making baby chicks, was rooster soup. However, I've just had another poultry surprise. This month my husband, who injured his knee many years ago by jumping out of a helicopter in Vietnam, was given a "rooster comb shot," an injection of a substance that his doctor said could relieve pain and postpone the knee replacement surgery for which Nat has been mentally preparing himself. When I mentioned this to some friends, one of them said that she, too, had been injected with rooster combs. I guess everybody's doing it. I wonder if we could grow roosters just for people's knees, the way we keep chickens just for eggs? I wonder if we could sell rooster combs to the pharmaceutical industry and make our fortune? But most of all, I wonder about the mysteries of poultry and the workings of fate. After forty years of keeping chickens, my husband ended up with roosters in his knee.

IN AND OUT OF
THE BUCKET

Some people keep a "bucket list" of things they would like to add to their life experience before they die. The Internet provides near-infinite suggestions for these bucket lists, including becoming a stand-up comedian, climbing the Eiffel Tower, having your artwork hang in a New York City art gallery, and owning an Armani suit.

I'm a bit wary of the whole idea. The image of filling a bucket, then kicking said bucket, has never appealed to me. I use buckets every day: I feed the chickens with buckets, carry water or grain to the sheep, dig up and dispose of weeds in the garden, and spread manure. This is my bucket list.

Moreover, I have a traumatic bucket-related memory from childhood. I went to a summer camp for girls on a lake in Maine, where they had "bucket races." First, we formed lines for teams, out at the end of the dock where the water was deep. The first person in each team was supposed to jump into the lake holding a galvanized tin bucket. She would swim out to a buoy, then turn and swim back to the dock, handing the bucket to the next person in her team's line.

I was eager to participate. When I was nine, I enjoyed obeying rules and following directions. I had learned to swim and dive pretty well, and I was all lined up and ready to go—in fact, I think I was first in line.

The one thing I had failed to understand was that because a bucket race involves swimming through water, you can only make progress if you hold the bucket by the bottom, with two hands. I dove in holding the bucket by the handle. The bucket filled instantly, dragging me straight to the bottom of the lake. Fortunately, a counselor dove in after me, pried my hand off the bucket's handle (I was afraid to let go—what if I lost the bucket?), and dragged me to safety.

Maybe that's my problem with bucket lists. For me, buckets are either full of troubling memories or smelly farm chores. As to lists, I feel as if I already have plenty going on right now. If anything, my bucket of experience is over-full. It may be time to take a few things out of it rather than putting more things in.

Many friends of my age are adding foreign travel to their lives in retirement, and loving their experiences. I, too, enjoyed the years when I traveled as a young girl long ago, with my family or on my own. I lived in Switzerland for one year and in France for another, did some traveling in Europe, spent a month in India, and later, a month in East Africa. But now, fifty years later, I seem to be staying put.

Aside from cutting back on foreign travel, I have given up certain other activities that have been part of my life since childhood. I stopped horseback riding after the last of our horses died. She was a gentle, gracious Lippitt Morgan mare, Dulcie, and she took good care of anyone who got up on her back. She moved along with an easy gait, never making a sudden move.

Dulcie was actually a kind of therapy horse for uneasy riders, and especially therapeutic for me. She came into my life at the end of a succession of horses and ponies of varying breeds and temperaments. One of them almost killed me. A beautiful young bay gelding named Hagarty, with a black mane and tail, he was affectionate in the barnyard but lively and skittish on our dirt road. One day in March when we were out together he shied at something—A leaf? A glimmer of ice on the roadside?—and then galloped wildly for home after dumping me onto the still-frozen ground, on my head.

Unfortunately, I wasn't wearing a helmet, so I spent ten days in the hospital and several weeks recovering at home. I continue to take daily medication for a seizure disorder that cropped up some time later, probably caused by an injury to the brain during that fall.

I thought I would never ride a horse again. Then I met Dulcie, the best-natured horse I have ever known. She lived with us until she died at the age of thirty, and gave birth to several foals over the course of the years. I don't think I will ever find another horse like her, and I won't try.

However, I do have a friend who decided that what she wanted most for her eightieth birthday was to try horseback riding for the first time. She loved it, and her experience made me think about getting back in the saddle again myself. I may wait until my own eightieth birthday, and I may not tell my children at all. I suspect there are a few things they have done in their lives without telling me.

I've given up downhill or Alpine skiing, too, now that all the children have grown up and left home. I have skied for most of my life, first with my parents and siblings from the time I was very young—six or seven—and throughout my young adulthood. I skied with my own kids during their school years in Vermont, chaperoning ski programs one afternoon a week at a local ski area that offers special rates to schools, and driving carpools with other parents on weekends. After the children had grown up, it seemed both expensive and lonely to ski all by myself on a mountain several miles from home when I could go out our kitchen door and ski with my husband on cross-country trails right here on the farm. Still, I dream about downhill skiing: the curve and sweep of my body moving down the slope, the cold freshness of wind whipping in my face, the freedom that feels like flying. I may not have given it up for good.

Something else that I may have stopped doing—though, again, I reserve the right to change my mind—is driving to New York City. I haven't driven to New York for a while now, five years at least, but when I was younger if I had to get there, or anywhere else, I always drove. It didn't matter what time of day it was, or what time of the year, or—within reason—what kind of weather or traffic I might encounter along the way. I just got in my car and I drove.

When first one and then the other of my daughters lived in New York City, I always drove to visit them: five-and-a-half hours south, first on Interstate 91 and then on I-95 to the Henry Hudson Bridge, over the bridge to the West Side Highway and on to 33

Carmine Street in Father Demo Square, near Bleecker Street in the West Village. My destination was a third-floor apartment where first Susannah and then her older sister Lizzy lived while they were going to college and graduate school respectively. That apartment would be unaffordable these days, I know, but back then, that's where everyone their age lived. It was a small but pleasant, light-filled apartment with a tiny kitchen/living area and a sleeping loft, just above a very good bakery. I remember two things about visiting that apartment: the wonderful smells that wafted upward and in through the windows; and the shapeless, almost unmanageable weight of the futon I helped to move up or down those flights of stairs each time a daughter moved in or out of the apartment. It was like carrying an unconscious walrus.

Now, both of my daughters are living in other places with their families: Susannah lives in Los Angeles, Lizzy in Vermont. Both are teachers. I don't know what happened to the futon.

My son Ben, more than a decade younger than his sisters, has lived in New York for several years, in Ridgewood, Queens. He commutes to work using subways and buses. Sometimes he rides his bicycle. For two years he worked as a bicycle messenger in Manhattan, which scared me a lot. He argued that the money was good, the exercise kept him fit, and it would have been much more dangerous to be a New York City firefighter or a police officer. I was very happy when he got another job.

On my trips to New York now, I drive south from my home only as far as White River Junction, a little less than an hour away. I park my car in the lot and take the Amtrak Vermonter all the way to Penn Station. The train journey takes about seven hours, but I relish every minute of it. I can't take as much stuff with me as I could if I drove my car, but if I drove I would pay for gas and would have the added expense of parking in New York. Besides, if I had room for more stuff, I just know there would be futons in my life again. No thanks.

People tell me that going to New York by car is faster and more efficient, that the bus is just as comfortable, and that there are quick, inexpensive commuter flights to the city. In short, other forms of transportation are better than the train.

I disagree. Nothing could be better than the train. When planning a New York trip, I happily reserve a seat for myself in Business

Class several weeks ahead of time—now, instead of driving anywhere, anytime, I plot out my movements in advance—and I travel quite economically. (Between my Amtrak Rewards Card and my Senior Discount, the railroad practically pays me to take the train.) As for comfort, what could be more comfortable than sitting quietly and watching the Connecticut River landscape go by, with the trees and the birds and the slow, peaceful length of the river for company? Further south, when the view becomes more industrial, I can read or write or get up and go to the dining car to get coffee and maybe a hot dog or a cheeseburger. They have salads and wraps, too, for passengers seeking healthier nourishment, but I'm not one of them. What's the fun of travel if I can't eat hot dogs?

I'd be glad to stay on the train longer than the seven hours it takes to get to New York. I like the special quality of the time a train offers, just the way it feels to be moving along on the rails. I didn't even mind the years when we had to go backwards for the stretch of the trip between Palmer, Massachusetts and Penn Station because of what my husband calls "trackage rights ineptitude." I enjoyed the oddly altered view. It doesn't hurt to have a change in perspective now and then.

Eventually, in the fullness of train time, I arrive in Penn Station and emerge onto the New York City streets. Still lulled by train rhythms, I stand in the taxi line in the rain. It is so often raining when I arrive in New York that I routinely come up the stairs out of Penn Station with my umbrella in hand, and am pleasantly surprised if the sun is shining.

My cab takes me north and across Central Park to 122 East 66th Street. This is the home of the Cosmopolitan Club, where I am a member like my mother and grandmother and aunts before me, as well as some of my contemporary cousins. The Cosmopolitan Club is the best part of staying in New York for me and for the other club ladies I know, though we may be embarrassed to admit it. A ladies club in New York? In the twenty-first century?

Why not? Staying in a New York hotel, which I've certainly done, too, is more expensive and less friendly, and the club members don't do any harm that I can see. My son—affectionately, I hope—calls them (well, us) "the frosted ladies," including in this description most of the women walking along Lexington Avenue between 50th and 80th Streets, with their handbags and umbrellas.

The Cosmopolitan Club was originally established between 1907 and 1909 as "The Club for Governesses," founded by women of means on behalf of "self-supporting women of education," who had no place to gather with friends on their days off. Later, the club expanded to include "a variety of self-supporting women," whether in education, the arts, or other areas of professional endeavor. These are very interesting women. My mother supported the candidacy of her close friend and editor Helen Wolff of Pantheon Books and Harcourt Brace Jovanovich years ago, and I recently attended a birthday party at the club for an old friend, "Clicker Training" proponent Karen Pryor. An author, a teacher, and a renowned animal trainer, Karen has trained dolphins and dogs with equally cheerful expertise and was formerly a Marine Mammal Commissioner in the US government.

Now I stay at the club whenever I visit New York. I luxuriate in a small room where the furniture and wallpaper, or the tastefully framed floral prints on off-white walls, are as familiar as if I had known them from childhood. I could be staying with my grandmother in New Jersey in 1953. The walrus-futon days are long gone.

In the morning, I have breakfast in a big, quiet dining room with several other women, all of us reading the *New York Times*. Someone comes to the table to take my order (scrambled eggs and bacon? hot croissants? muesli with fruit?) and pours hot coffee into my cup at well-timed intervals. This is my idea of heaven. New York visits can stay in the bucket.

I may need to discard some of my other activities, though many of them are deeply entangled in my basic nature. In addition to my mother, with her well-known aviation and literary accomplishments, I also had a grandmother and several energetic aunts who were what my mother called "committee women," meaning that they served on boards of trustees. My maternal grandmother, Elizabeth Cutter Morrow, graduated from Smith College in 1896, was president of the Smith College Alumnae Association, a trustee of the Board, and, ultimately—although she never held the official title—the first female head of Smith College. My mother's older sister, Elisabeth, an educator and an early advocate for the education of young children, established what she called "The Little School" (now the Elisabeth Morrow School) in her hometown of Englewood, New Jersey. Her younger sister, Constance Morrow Morgan, my Aunt Con, was also devoted to educational and philanthropic causes throughout her life.

Once I start to list the things I do, I have to admit that my own "committee woman" life is full—maybe over-full, like that summer camp bucket, though I haven't yet drowned. I have two committee-woman lives. Here in Vermont, I volunteer for our local library, the St. Johnsbury Athenaeum, and I serve on the board of Back Roads Reading, a group that offers readings by nationally known poets and writers in the summer. I lead a monthly writers' program at the St. Johnsbury Senior Center. I also serve as a trustee of the Vermont Arts Council. In New York, I am a director of the Harry Frank Guggenheim Foundation, founded by an old friend of my father and devoted to the study of aggression and violence. I'm also the vice president of the Elisabeth Reeve Morrow Morgan Foundation, set up by my mother, my Aunt Con, and my Uncle Dwight long ago to honor their sister Elisabeth.

That foundation meeting takes place once a year at the Cosmopolitan Club itself and includes members of the Englewood community, local parents and supporters of the Elisabeth Morrow School, and three descendants of the founders—at this time, one Lindbergh (me), one Morrow (Anne Fulenwider, granddaughter of founder Dwight Morrow Jr.), and one Morgan (Elisabeth Morgan Pendleton, daughter of "Aunt Con"). I listen to very interesting people, I take notes, and I cast my vote to give money to the school. This duty stays in the bucket.

Then there is the Charles A. and Anne Morrow Lindbergh Foundation, where I serve in an honorary capacity now, though I was a director from the time of the organization's founding in 1977 until 2003. The organization was established through a collaboration between the Explorer's Club in New York City and the World Wildlife Fund at the time of the fiftieth anniversary of the flight of the *Spirit of St. Louis* from New York to Paris. Although the name changed after my mother's death to "The Charles A. and Anne Morrow Lindbergh Foundation," the organization was never a "Foundation" in the sense of the Rockefeller or Guggenheim Foundations, not founded or funded by the family from which it took its name. Rather, the Lindbergh Foundation was and is supported mainly by large and small donors throughout the country.

For many years, we honored with an annual Lindbergh Award individuals whose life's work showed the "balance" my father envisioned: people like Jacques Cousteau, explorer, scientist, and conservationist of the sea, and Dr. Paul MacCready, aircraft designer and pioneer of human-powered flight and environmentally responsible design. We also offered Lindbergh Grants each year in amounts up to $10,580, the actual cost of building the *Spirit of St. Louis* airplane in 1927. These grants were awarded in many different fields, but always with reference to "balance" between technology and the environment. Recently, the foundation initiated a program called "Air Shepherd" that uses aerial drones to successfully identify and combat poaching of elephants and rhinos in South Africa, Zimbabwe, and Malawi, with increasing interest from other parts of the continent.

After so many years of involvement, it would be too difficult to remove myself from the work of the Lindbergh Foundation entirely, but I now think of myself as an elder stateswoman in the organization, offering my support and a family connection, but not interfering with day-to-day operations.

The Lindbergh Foundation, the Elisabeth Reeve Morrow Morgan Foundation, the Harry Frank Guggenheim Foundation, the Vermont Arts Council, Back Roads Reading, the Friends of the St. Johnsbury Athenaeum. These days, for me, that sounds like a pretty full bucket. Still, most of them only meet once or twice a year. The others meet more often, quarterly or monthly, but happily some of these meetings take place by phone, so I don't even have to leave the house to attend.

Phone meetings, in fact, help me to remove one habit from my bucket that I have been concerned about for some time. This is something I call Rushing Around, which involves getting in my car and driving here and there to do things that aren't very important. Aside from wasting gasoline and threatening the health of the planet, Rushing Around gives me a fractured, distracted feeling and tires me out. I'm hoping to do much less of this in future.

The other habit I want to give up is a kind of blundering Helpfulness that has afflicted me for many decades. I'm always trying to help. There's nothing wrong with the impulse, which is after all an outgrowth of Good Manners and Courtesy and Thinking of Others, lessons I was taught, and taught my children, and, I hope, they will teach theirs.

My problem is that I frequently rush to help before considering what kind of help, if any, is needed. Not long ago, I was walking up Eastern Avenue in St. Johnsbury, Vermont, on a beautiful day, and I happened upon a man sitting halfway in and halfway out of the front passenger seat of a car. A woman standing near him was struggling with a collapsible walker, something the man clearly needed to use to make his way along the sidewalk.

They needed my help! I told them so. "Oh, let me help you," I said, kindly removing the walker from the woman's grasp and firmly opening it—click!—so that it was fully operational. I smiled at the two people I had assisted, and they smiled back at me. Then the woman said, a little bewildered, "Thank you so much, but actually I was trying to close it. We have to go home."

I hastily un-helped them again (closed the walker, apologized) and went on my way. As I walked up the street to the corner, I could still hear the man chuckling.

There will be some things that will never come out of the bucket. I'll never stop reading, I know that, on whatever technology I may use to read (Audio books? Kindle devices with a fifty-point font?), and I will keep on writing forever, using whatever technology exists.

But other things that I think of as part of my day-to-day existence, it turns out, might be more negotiable. The year after I had brain surgery to remove a non-cancerous tumor, I needed a lot of help. I was very fortunate in the outcome and I recovered well, but I was tired for months afterwards and had trouble with balance (precarious) and with blinking (almost constant, for a while). Also, until the right combination of medications was established, I had seizures. These came in the form of a kind of blinking, very literal absence of mind, over a period of seconds or minutes. I don't remember this because that's the nature of seizures, but other people certainly do. (I sometimes kept right on doing whatever I was doing before the seizure occurred, once knitting a full row of stitches while—I guess—not "with it" in any other way.)

I did not drive for a full year, so others had to drive me wherever I needed to go. Everybody I met inquired about my health, offered support, and tried to help as much as possible. I found this very touching and thoughtful of them, and at the same time, completely disconcerting. I was the helper, wasn't I? Not the one who needed help! How could I be in this position?

Because of that year, I realize this is another habit I will have to discard as time goes on: thinking that I don't ever need help myself. So far, I'm not making a whole lot of headway.

Oh well: my time of needing more help will come when it comes. Along with it, I realize, will come the time when I can no longer drive, not just for a year but forever. I don't think I'm ready to think about it quite yet. No Rushing Around *at all?*

Being me, I can't help wondering whether I couldn't still drive around the farm in or on some vehicle, even if I am not driving on town roads in my car. Maybe I will drive the John Deere "Gator," which looks like a golf cart, only my husband uses it to lead the sheep up to the high pastures in the morning and down again at night. This is a cheerful-looking process (unless it's raining—soggy husband, even soggier sheep), though not fast, because the Gator and the sheep alike move at a stately pace, with the sheep enticed to movement at all only by the bucket of grain stashed in the open back of the vehicle. Nat shakes the bucket vigorously to show the flock its contents (this is one of our sweeter-smelling farm buckets), then the sheep follow the vehicle, and the dog follows them to lend encouragement, and they all get where they need to go.

Today, I rarely drive the Gator; after all, it's a farm vehicle, and my husband needs it. However, years from today, when I have become completely accustomed to <u>not</u> doing other things—not skiing, not horseback riding, not driving to New York, not Rushing Around, not *helping*—I have my eye on that Gator.

In my advanced old age or infirmity, I don't know how well I'll be able to move around, but I'm sure I'll manage to carry out this plan . . . I'll go outdoors and (with the help of a stepladder, or maybe—Hey!—an upside-down bucket) I'll climb on my John Deere Elder-Vehicle, and I'll drive freely, gleefully, fearlessly, and joyfully all over the farm.

MADISON

In 2014, to my complete surprise, I was invited to deliver a lecture at the University of Wisconsin in Madison. The Department of Mechanical Engineering has an annual "Lindbergh Lecture" because my father briefly attended that university in the early 1920s. It must have seemed reasonable to ask me to come to Madison one year and give the Lindbergh Lecture.

I wanted to accept, but because I didn't want to disappoint the audience I thought I had better talk to somebody from the university first. As an English major with little science or technology background, I was not in any way qualified to speak to these people, I told Roxy Engelstadt, a mechanical engineering professor at the university and a key member of the Lindbergh Lecture planning group. Roxy explained cheerfully that I didn't need mechanical engineering credentials to give the talk. All I needed was my family history and my thoughts and memories of my parents. I have those, so I accepted.

I thought I might learn more about my father as a young man if I went to Madison. I might learn more about my grandmother too. When my father went to college in 1920, his mother went with him. I had always wondered why.

In my own college years, during the 1960s, Madison was mainly associated in my mind with anti-Vietnam War protests and political activism. Forty years before that, my father had been moved from school to school, back and forth across the country, in order to live with each of his estranged parents for some part of the year. The University of Wisconsin was one of the few schools he attended for longer than a year. In high school, though he did well in physics and mechanical drawing, he was not a good student. He found it almost impossible to be interested in schoolwork at any time. His own father had been elected to the US House of Representatives in 1907 and had spent little time in Little Falls, Minnesota since that year. So at the age of fifteen, my father was running the family farm he loved and going to high school as well. My father rode his bicycle to and from school every day in decent weather, or walked there and back in the sub-zero Minnesota winters he used to tell us about in terrifying detail. Sometimes he also came home for lunch.

His mother had been a teacher, and perhaps it was her influence that kept him going to school at all. I hate to think of my father moving from school to school and place to place during his earlier childhood: it is so hard for any child to adjust to a new school system socially and academically even once, let alone a dozen times.

I didn't know until I was an adult that my father's parents had separated while he was still very young. For much of his childhood he lived alone with his mother. They spent the winters in Washington, DC, during the years when his father first served in Congress, they visited his maternal grandparents in Detroit at various points during the year, and spent summers on the farm in Minnesota.

He talked about his parents as individuals: "my mother" or "my father," not "my parents." He did not mention their literal, physical separation, though his parents had established separate residences by the time he was seven years old. They did not divorce because of possible damage to C. A. Lindbergh's reputation with his constituents. C. A. and Evangeline were committed to cooperation in the raising of their son, but neither of them managed to instill in the boy any love for formal schooling.

My father wrote in his short memoir of farm life, *Boyhood on the Upper Mississippi*, about the winters of 1917–1918, the only time he actually lived on the farm during the school year. His mother and her brother, Charles Land, whom we children knew later as "Uncle," had returned to Minnesota with their own mother, then dying of breast cancer. My father tried to balance a full load of daily farm chores with his high school classes. Returned to the farm after school, outdoor duties always presented themselves as both more immediately essential and more appealing than homework. But once farm chores were done and he'd eaten supper, he was too tired to turn to his textbooks. His grades were usually poor.

He finally dropped out of school altogether, rescued by World War I. At a school assembly in late winter, the principal announced to the students that since food was so necessary in the war effort, any student could leave school to work on a farm and receive complete, full, academic credit, just as though he'd gone to class and passed his exams. My father leapt at the opportunity, devoting himself full-time to the farm, only returning to the school to collect his diploma.

Though my father continued to farm after armistice was declared in November 1918, he was becoming increasingly interested in the new technological era opening up all over the world. During the war, he had become fascinated by the aerial exploits of pilots Baron von Richthofen and Eddie Rickenbacker, and dreamed of having a plane of his own. He applied to the University of Wisconsin's engineering department, was accepted, and arrived in Madison in September of 1920 on the twin-cylinder Excelsior motorcycle with which he had traveled the rural roads of Minnesota selling milking machines to local farmers. This time he rode 350 miles to college from his home in Little Falls, arriving after classes had already begun.

I knew none of this history when I was growing up, but I was aware that my father did not seem interested in his children's school or school-supporting activities: no class programs, no school plays, no teachers conferences, no graduations. Our mother did all of that. I assumed that our father stayed home—when, in fact, he *was* home— because he avoided public gatherings due to his mistrust of The Press. My mother, on the other hand, was a diplomat's daughter who, though shy by nature, knew what to do in large groups of people and had been trained to public service. She was a daughter and sister of educators, and respected her own education and ours.

Indeed, my father had an oddly dismissive attitude when it came to the whole scholastic enterprise. When I was in elementary school in the 1950s and it was time for report cards to be issued, the teachers gave their students a letter for the grade—A, B, C, D or F—and a number for Effort—1, 2, or 3—to indicate whether the teacher believed the student was working according to his or her ability or simply getting by without trying. If, on my report card, I got an A #1 in Reading, for instance, I came home ecstatic. An A #1 meant that my achievement and my effort in class were both excellent. My father, though, after looking at my report card, laughed and said that he would have been more impressed if I had received a grade of A #5, because that would mean that my achievement was both excellent and effortless. Huh? I didn't get it.

My mother probably said, "Oh, Charles!"

I concluded that my father must have hated school when he was my age, the way many of the others in my class, especially the boys, hated school now. On the other hand, it was clear to me that my father was really smart: how else could he have done all the things he did, and written all those books?

Years later, I found a piece of the answer in his first book, *We*, where he wrote about his studies at the College of Engineering at the University of Wisconsin. "The long hours of study at college were very trying for me. I had spent most of my life outdoors and had never before found it necessary to spend more than a part of my time in study."[1]

Aha! He had not "found it necessary" to study. He was one of those children who could survive in school without paying much attention to his books or his teachers. When I was a teacher myself, I had a few of those students in my classes. They were often the ones who could do other, non-academic things brilliantly—paint wondrous scenes from their imaginations and draw lifelike animals from nature and memory, tell stories the whole class gathered around to hear, act brilliantly in the class play. They were often difficult, and they always won my heart.

My father wasn't like those children, though; at least, not when I knew him. He was well organized, self-disciplined, under tight self-control, sometimes grimly stern, but sometimes suddenly cheerful, lighting up the room with the grin that people talked about from his "Lindy" days as a young man.

I didn't see him as an artist, not at all. Still, with my father there were always surprises. I remember a small painting that hung over the desk in his study. It showed an apple orchard in full bloom, and was to my eye of the time very beautiful. In the hazy way that recollection sometimes comes, I can see myself standing next to him as he sits at his desk, and asking him who painted that painting. He told me very matter-of-factly that he did.

As an adult I wondered whether I had dreamed the whole childhood encounter, and the painting too. There was such color and light in that painted orchard on its hillside, with every tree a cloud of blossoms, pink standing out against green.

I finally thought to ask my brother Land about it. Land often remembers family history more accurately than I do. Was there ever such a painting? Did our father really paint it? Land wrote back:

> Yes, your recollection is correct. I have the painting hanging here in my office, and am looking at it right now. And yes, it is as you describe. My understanding, based on what I can remember from what Father told me, and as well something written in Mother's diaries, is that this painting was done while they lived on Long Island. He must have been on a hill looking down toward Long Island Sound (maybe from a porch?) through what I believe are three oak or possibly elm trees, at the orchard down below and on to a sandy beach and then the sunset beyond. All very meticulously done, which is what impressed me so much. When I asked him about one of the branches hanging at a slightly odd angle, he responded by saying that it hung exactly as depicted . . . I bet, and I also bet that it hasn't dared to make a move ever since.

My brother's reassurance that the painting was real also confirmed what I remember about our father. Though he never had seemed to me to be the kind of person who would create such a painting, he did create it, and he claimed it in his characteristic manner. He stood by every brushstroke.

We called our parents Mother and Father, not Mom and Dad. We still refer to them that way. I don't know whether it was a formality that came from my mother's family—though I seem to remember her referring to her father in letters to her sisters as "Daddy"—or a remnant from my father's family roots in Sweden, where a child would refer to a father as "Far" and a mother as "Mor." In Swedish, a grandmother's name depended on whether she was the mother's mother or the father's mother. Our Lindbergh grandmother, Evangeline, was our father's mother, and we always called her "Farmor," even though she was not from the Swedish side of the family but the other side, the Lands and the Lodges, who came from Detroit.

Farmor had only one child, my father, and was very close to him. She even lived with her son when he attended the University of Wisconsin. She traveled to Madison by train in the fall of 1920, arriving there a few weeks before my father did. Evangeline had lived with her son and without her husband for so many years that it must have seemed completely natural to her to move to Madison when my father was to attend college there. She found work as a substitute physical science teacher in a local junior high school and rented an apartment for herself and my father on the top floor of a building not far from the campus. Her estranged husband, now living in Florida and attempting to engage in real estate transactions, was able to send them fifty dollars a month, which did not cover the seventy dollars monthly rent or other expenses needed for the support of his wife and son. Evangeline worked because she had to.

When I visited Madison in 2014 for the Lindbergh Lecture, Roxy and Mary Jane, the sister of a friend from Vermont, and Mary Jane's husband, John, took me to see the apartment where my father and grandmother had lived at 35 North Mills Street. We didn't go inside, but I was glad to look up at the third-floor apartment and to imagine my father living in it as a young man.

Looking at the building didn't really tell me much about my grandmother, but very little that I've learned about her has done that. I remember my Lindbergh grandmother slightly, in every sense. For me, she was a thin body outlined under the covers of her bed; I can't remember her standing up or walking or moving at all, though my older brothers can. I recall a pale face against a pillow, with wavy gray-white hair and a small moist smile, what I thought of as the smile of a very tired person, as indeed it may have been. This is all I have in terms of direct memory, though I've gleaned bits and pieces about her from books and from conversations over the years. My grandmother did not get along well with her stepdaughters, my father's older half-sisters Lillian and Eva. When I met Eva in Minnesota following my father's death, she was bitter about her stepmother. She believed that Evangeline had been cruel to her father and had actually caused Lillian's death with her rages and her unpredictable behavior. (Never a strong child, Lillian had died of tuberculosis in 1916.)

I never heard about his mother's behavior from my father at all. I learned about her favorite flowers (iris, nasturtium, purple violets) and her cooking (home-baked bread and pies, sweet corn, vegetables from the garden) and that she was reputed to be "the most beautiful girl in Ann Arbor" when she was living in Michigan before she decided to travel west to Minnesota and teach chemistry in the high school in Little Falls. I also learned that her teaching career in Little Falls was cut short by a dispute with the superintendent of schools, attributed by my father to "my mother's flashing Irish temper," but he didn't talk about rages or cruelty, ever.

My mother, if I asked her, referred to my Lindbergh grandmother as "troubled," and suggested that Evangeline Lindbergh could have used some kind of "help," meaning psychotherapy. Still, all the letters to her mother-in-law that I have seen in my mother's books and in the archives are affectionate and appreciative. The two women must have had a fairly harmonious relationship, whatever their private thoughts and feelings may have been.

"I think she got a bad rap," A. Scott Berg, my father's biographer, once said to me of my grandmother. He describes Evangeline Lindbergh as a feminist, an educator, and a strong spirit—with, yes, some possible chemical imbalance (inner turmoil, frustration, rages), but also with great integrity and stamina. Her husband, my grandfather, comes across as a difficult character. He was handsome and powerful, with a dry sense of humor and appealing idealism, and it is certain that his children were all very fond of him. Still, C. A. Lindbergh had trouble managing his finances and supporting his family, and a tendency to become involved with other women.

My father's half-sister Eva despised her stepmother but adored her father. "Uncle" clearly was devoted to his sister, Evangeline. My own father, though his two parents were distanced from one another for most of his life, deeply loved them both.

I have the feeling that my Lindbergh grandmother and grandfather were bad for each other, as some couples can be, for reasons that can be explained in many ways but which are ultimately unfathomable. Yet the more I learn about them, the more I think I, too, would have loved them both, as my father did.

My father for some time had been doing a man's job of running the Minnesota farm and tending to animals and machinery. By 1920, he was not a typical college student. Even in Madison, with an off-campus home made familiar and comfortable by his mother, and with engineering as his focus, my father did not apply himself to schoolwork. Instead, he spent time traveling the roads of rural Wisconsin on his motorcycle, making friends with other motorcycle enthusiasts at the school like fellow engineering student Delos Dudley, and engaging in rifle and pistol shooting. He found a place on the ROTC rifle and pistol teams during his freshman year, where he excelled—indeed, he remained a skilled marksman throughout his lifetime—but he never did catch up with his engineering studies.

During my visit to Madison, I stayed at the Edgewater Hotel, an elegant establishment dating from the 1940s. I was very comfortable and enjoyed my stay a great deal, but it would be hard to imagine any place that would remind me less of my father. When we traveled with him in the 1950s, he always liked to stay in out-of-the-way, family-run hotels, somewhat like today's bed-and-breakfasts, if less self-consciously decorative. He referred to these places as "good third-class hotels," which seemed to me a contradiction in terms, but my father always knew exactly what he meant, and just what he liked. I don't think I could have persuaded him to stay at the Edgewater, but I'd go back any time.

For dinner on my first night, I went to Roxy's home on the farm where she lives with her husband, Ed Lovell, a retired professor in the mechanical engineering department. They have about 140 acres of farmland that grows corn and soybeans, a place that her family has owned for generations. The Engelstadts were Norwegian immigrants, not unlike my Swedish family in Minnesota. The very first wooden buildings are still on the property, including a tiny shack with uneven clapboards and no windows: a pioneer home.

The place where Ed and Roxy live now is something else entirely, a spacious Frank Lloyd Wright-inspired building of stone and glass, featuring soaring ceilings and beautiful wood trim. Over the fireplace were fossil fish embedded in expanses of what looked like marble. "Three million years old," Roxy said, with an intense blue-eyed look at the fish and a smile for me. She and Ed designed much of their home, and they live in it with two golden retrievers.

I spoke with many people from the university, and was especially interested to meet Professor Tim Osswald, who would give the introduction to my lecture the next day. He is half-Colombian, half-German—his parents fled from the Nazis just before World War II—and he speaks several languages.

My father, despite his extensive travels, never learned to speak a foreign language at all. He claimed he could make himself understood anywhere in the world. He demonstrated this to us in Austria once when he wanted an egg for breakfast, pretending to be a chicken by crooking his elbows to make "wings," then flapping and clucking with gusto. It worked, and it delighted the proprietor of the inn where we stayed.

Certainly, he learned no foreign languages at the University of Wisconsin in Madison, and according to his record he seems to have learned little else, either. A letter to my grandmother from my father's university advisor does not spell my father's name correctly but otherwise gives what I'm sure is an accurate account of his dismal scholastic record at the end of the first semester of his sophomore year:

Machine Design 1 . . . . Failure
Mathematics 52 . . . . Failure
Physics 51 . . . . Incomplete
Shop 6 88
Shop 13 88

The letter finishes with this sentence:

On account of the above poor record the Sophomore Advisor Committee decided on February 2 that Carl should be dropped from the University.[2]

My father did not mention his grades or the above letter when he wrote about leaving college in *The Spirit of St. Louis*: "When I was a sophomore at the University of Wisconsin, I decided to give up my course in mechanical engineering, and learn to fly."[3]

His mother, who had always been concerned about the dangers of flying, did not follow him to flying school in Nebraska. She left Wisconsin and went back to Detroit to teach chemistry at Cass Technical High School, where she remained until she retired in 1942.

My father learned to fly at the Nebraska Air Craft Corporation in Lincoln, making his first flight on April 22, 1922, at the age of twenty. Later, he spent time barnstorming, doing aerial acrobatics, wing walking, and parachute jumping throughout Midwestern and Western states with other pioneer aviators, including Bud Gurney, a young Nebraska pilot who became a lifelong friend. My father then worked as a flying instructor in St. Louis, eventually enrolling in the Army Air Service School at Brooks Field and graduating in 1925 as a second lieutenant in the United States Army Air Service Reserve— this time, at the top of his class.

When I visited the University of Wisconsin for the Lindbergh Lecture, I knew my father hadn't been a good student during his time there. Nonetheless, when I spoke at Madison, I talked about the important part I thought that his experience at the University had played in his subsequent career. If nothing else, he confirmed in Madison what he must have felt throughout his childhood: that he greatly preferred an outdoor, physical life to an indoor and studious one, and that he passionately wanted to fly.

In his introduction to my talk, Tim Osswald persuasively argued that my father, in his post-curricular activities, had proved himself a worthy alumnus and a more than worthy engineering student, college grades notwithstanding. He had fully earned academic honors, though not in an academic manner, through the planning, organization, meticulous design work, and execution of the 1927 flight from New York to Paris in the *Spirit of St. Louis*. Dr. Osswald felt it entirely appropriate not only that my father returned to UW-Madison in 1927 during his "Guggenheim Fund Tour" around the United States to promote commercial aviation, but also that in 1928 he received an honorary doctorate. University President Glenn Frank called the degree the university's "Legion d'Honneur," and said to my father, "The University of Wisconsin awards you its highest honorary degree . . . for what you have done . . ."

From the reports and the photographs I have seen of the events, my father came back to Wisconsin alone following the flight that made him famous. His mother did not accompany him. I still wonder what she must have thought, the woman who had made him a home and supported him during the year and a half that he attended college but did not study. I wonder whether she responded the way I did. I am her granddaughter, after all, and a former teacher, and I, too, loved the unpredictable, often bewildering person who was her son and my father. I cannot help but be amazed when I think of him receiving an honorary doctorate at the University of Wisconsin, Madison, six years after he had been asked to leave in the middle of his sophomore year because of failing grades. It is true that by June of 1928 he was accustomed to receiving honors and awards. He had received hundreds of medals, trophies, proclamations, and gifts from countries around the world in tribute to his New York to Paris flight. From his own country, he had received both the Congressional Medal of Honor and the Distinguished Flying Cross. Honorary degrees, too, already had been presented to him by Northwestern University, Washington University in St. Louis, St. Joseph's College in Philadelphia, New York University, and Princeton University.

If I had been his mother, I would have insisted that he accept the invitation from the one university he had actually attended, regardless of the quality of his performance there as a student. However, I like to think that he went back to Madison willingly and without anyone's insistence. He was a courteous man by nature, and he might have been glad to visit the campus and see old friends like Delos Dudley. He may have been pleased, too, to have his success recognized in a setting where he had known failure.

To this day, though, whenever I think of my father on the podium in Madison in 1928 in his cap and gown, I remember not only his difficulties at every school he ever attended, but also all the disparaging things he used to say about formal education in general.

Then, as sometimes happens when I find myself thinking about my father, I suddenly remember him clearly, just the man himself as

I knew him. He was a complicated person and I'm not sure I ever really understood him or ever will, but once in a while he's there, just the way he always was, the father I knew and loved. There is a kind of simplicity in his felt presence, so that I can let go of everything I've been thinking and pondering and puzzling over. When this happens I take a deep breath, and shake my head slowly, and smile.

ICE CUBES IN THE ORCHIDS

For best results, don't water orchids, instead give them ice cubes: one ice cube once a week. Or maybe it's two ice cubes—I can't exactly remember. Essentially, it's a matter of taking the ice cube tray from the freezer on Saturday, distributing one or two cubes in each pot, then forgetting all about it until the following weekend. In any case, the few of these exotic plants I have, given to me by friends and family members, are all still alive. Each year, they produce long stems adorned with subtly pink, white-and-purple, or deep maroon blossoms, and the flowers last a month or more even in the depths of winter. I don't know if this has anything to do with the ice cubes, but I'm not changing my system. Why take chances?

I love household hints. I've gathered them for decades, from relatives and friends, but also from passing acquaintances. A mother of another child in my daughter's playgroup, back when my daughter was still young enough to be in a playgroup, told me that if I put a slice of bread into a box of hardened brown sugar and left it for a few days, the sugar would get all soft and crumbly again. The first time I tried this, I was self-conscious and convinced it wouldn't work. When it did, transforming the dark brown sugar clump in its box on my shelf into a delightfully refreshed, softened version of itself, I thought it was a miracle. No more chipping away at hard brown lumps when I wanted to have milk and brown sugar on my cereal. I just tucked in a slice of bread—white bread or brown bread work equally well—and that was it.

Over the years, I've amassed a library of books filled with these tidbits and advice, dating from many eras of housekeeping. Peg Bracken's *The I Hate to Housekeep Book* from 1962 is one of my favorites. She points out right away all the things the mid-twentieth-century American housewife did not need to bother with: ironing sheets, pajamas, or her husband's handkerchiefs; polishing furniture; cleaning pastry-brush bristles ("I have been embarrassed by many things in my life, but never by my pastry-brush bristles."). When I first discovered Peg, I gladly took up her precepts such as "Keep this in mind. Never let your furniture get the upper hand."[4] I relished the stories that transform housework into something much less mundane, like the one about the woman who enlivened her housewifely routine by regularly doing all her housework naked.

I'm not so crazy about the books of that same time period which suggested that a woman could improve her marriage by greeting her husband at the end of his working day (no mention of *her* working day, of course) wearing nothing but high heels and perfume. On the other hand, I also don't much care for the magazine articles urging women to do their housework in elaborate protective garb. One suggested costume was a thirty-gallon lawn-and-leaf trash bag with holes cut out for head and hands. Back then, and now, I couldn't really see myself in either of the roles implied here: Housewife as hooker? Housewife as animated garbage bag? In any case, my husband and I were both working full time in those days, so we just did the best we could with the housework together, on weekends. When I felt guilty I read Peg Bracken and ironed as little as possible.

Household hints from even earlier generations enthrall me too. According to *Putnam's Household Handbook* from 1916, "A weak solution of alum will revive the colors of a faded carpet after a thorough sweeping."[5] I don't really know what alum is—I have read that this substance is used as an ingredient in baking powder and as a crisping agent in the production of pickles—and I have no idea how I'd buy alum in the twenty-first century, but if our local dry cleaning establishment ever goes out of business, God forbid, maybe I'll give it a try.

Much as I love books of household hints from any era, the best suggestions I have received come from the people who are living along with me here and now. The advice most often, though not always, comes from women, and over the years it has changed. The best advice, the kind that I have treasured for a lifetime, goes much farther and deeper than all the household hints, into the realm of shared wisdom about love and loss, childrearing and marriage, birth and death, the whole of the complex human territory we must navigate during our lives.

Childbirth was the most intense, exhilarating, and exhausting experience of my life. I would have added that it was also the most frightening and painful experience too, except that the sensations of fear and pain I encountered at the beginning of my labor turned at some point into overwhelming *process*, something as inevitable as a river in full flood, completely beyond my control. On the waves of this force I was carried, if not oblivious to all other sensations then unable to respond to them until the process was completed, and by then I had a beautiful baby. The result was worth everything that came before.

I wasn't at all sure I would ever have another child. During the first dazed weeks I concluded that birth was a miracle, just as I'd been told, but the work involved was much too hard for the likes of me.

Then my neighbor, a mother of four, came to visit me. She admired the baby and she listened to what I said about the experience. She didn't say much in response, but what she did say stayed with me.

"Oh, you'll forget all of that," she said. "It changes." She was right. After childbirth, something happens to the mother, not only at the time but also in memory and in repetition.

For some women, and I was one of those, childbirth takes the body to the very edge of one's physical and emotional being, even over that edge. There is some internal separation as the body gives itself over to the experience and the mind is left behind. By the time the mind catches up again, thoughts and instincts are turning toward the baby, away from the birth experience. The tumult recedes, the child is the only thing that matters.

I have given birth four times. In each case I thought to myself immediately afterwards, even in the midst of my happiness at the baby's arrival, "Well, I don't want to go through *that* again," and yet within weeks—or even days—I began to think about having more children. My neighbor was right: you forget; it changes. I always looked forward to the birth of the next child, and even now, as a grandmother of four, if I could have another baby (and I dream about this sometimes, crazy as it may seem), I hope I would have the sense not do it—but I know I would be tempted.

My neighbor's wisdom was a message. I could do, had done, this thing, childbirth, just as she and so many others had done it. I now belonged to the great mass of women who had given birth over the centuries. We were a community, with our individual labors and our collective experiences, with our beloved children, with all the words we have offered to each other to ease the way.

There are messages for dying, too. Everyone dies. Nobody knows beforehand how you are supposed to do it. "What do I do, hold my breath?" a friend's father complained to her at the very end of his life.

We don't hear about the experience of dying in the same way we hear about giving birth, because you can't have a conversation with someone who has just died. Still, people who are dying do speak of the experience as it is happening. In one of my mother's last conversations with my father, he said of his own death, "It's not far away . . . It's just right here."

For me there was enormous reassurance in that message. He was saying that death was not the vast black hole of emptiness that I had imagined as a child, not a great chasm of nothingness outside of life and alien to it. Instead, he felt, death was a familiar place nearby, a resting place. He made it sound like a comfortable armchair by the fire.

My mother also told my brother Land that when my father was dying he said to her during a quiet period following a struggle for breath, "I am not afraid, but my body is afraid."

A few years ago I was one of several people who took turns sitting with a ninety-eight-year-old friend at the very end of her life. She had been failing steadily and was expected to die within a matter of days or even hours. She had been unable to see or hear well for some time, but she had always been a talker, so she kept right on talking.

Because her breathing was becoming more and more difficult,

she would speak only in light gasps as she exhaled. She had been given some pain medication, but at one point I could still hear her saying "hurt," "hurt," "hurt," with her out-breaths, and once, clearly, the whispering complaint, "Suffer . . . why?"

It was hard to listen to what she was saying and not be able to help her. I was relieved when she got stronger medication to ease the pain. Later, though, she began to repeat the word "scared" in the same little puffs of breath. She spoke very softly now, but the word was unmistakable.

Her priest came, then her doctor. Their presence seemed to relieve her fear. Soon her family arrived, too, after a long trip from a distant state. It was time for me to leave. I took with me my own unsettled feelings, but also my friend's absolute honesty about her own dying. That truth, with all its difficulty, was her message.

Just now, more than at other times in my life, I have been close to people who are entering or leaving the world: old friends dying, grandchildren arriving. People get born and die regularly, after all. What I've found is that to be present at a birth is uplifting, and to be present at a death can be uplifting in another way, as long as one can be open to the truth within it, whatever that may be each time.

I think of the last time I saw my father, the summer of 1974. I visited him at the Columbia-Presbyterian Medical Center in New York City, only a few days before my mother and brothers made the arrangements, at his request, to fly him to the island of Maui, where he wished to spend his last days and to be buried in the little churchyard near their home in Kipahulu.

I remember that at the hospital he and I spoke about air conditioning, which he claimed he disliked, even though it was the middle of a hot summer in New York and I, for one, wasn't sorry that the hospital used it. I don't remember what else we talked about, but I know that we sat for a while silently, and I noticed that one of his blue pads of airmail paper was on the table with a few words written on it in pencil, in his handwriting. I looked over and read this phrase, "I know there is infinity outside ourselves. I wonder if there is an infinity within us, as well."

I don't think he was asking a question. It was an observation, a message passed on to me, even if he didn't know I would ever read it.

My mother-in-law died at the age of ninety-six, and during her last thirty years she lived in a large white pre-Revolutionary house in New Ipswich, New Hampshire. The house had several staircases "and seven fireplaces," as she liked to point out to visitors. It also had many rooms filled with inherited family furniture, paintings, china, and silver, but no other people at all.

That she lived alone worried not only her friends and relatives, but also her doctor. My mother-in-law, however, was repelled by the notion of an assisted living residence and rejected the idea of having a caregiver live with her. A few local friends looked in on her regularly, and her housekeeper came in several days a week.

It was the housekeeper who found my mother-in-law in bed on the last morning of her life. She called 911 and my husband, and the ambulance arrived quickly with two EMTs, who rushed upstairs with a stretcher.

My mother-in-law roused herself enough to look at the first of the EMTs who entered the room, and then said very clearly, "It's been a long time since I've had such a handsome young man in my bedroom."

As far as we know, those were her last words.

My own mother did not say very much during the last years of her life, especially toward the end. I don't remember what her last words were, or even if she had any. She left some written messages around the house for a while, in her now shaky handwriting on various pieces of paper, each message saying more or less the same thing: "I am dying, but peacefully. Tell my children." At the time we found these notes she did not seem particularly peaceful. She was both physically and mentally fragile, quite often seemed worried or agitated but could not tell us why, and a few times I was startled that she seemed to think I was her younger sister, Con, who had died a year or two earlier.

A few weeks before her death, my mother was weaker and calmer. She would lie in bed and study her hands. I could see her lifting one hand up in the air to hold it before her eyes and study it, turning it over gracefully to look at it from every angle. Then she would put it down again and lift up the other one. My children used to do the same thing when they were babies, in their cribs, and I loved to watch them doing it.

It was midwinter in Vermont when my mother died. The snow was falling, there were birds on the branch of a tree just outside her window, everything was quiet. My mother was ninety-four years old and resting in her bed most of the time. Aside from watching over her, as her caregivers were doing, and spending time with her, as her family did, there was not very much to be done. What there was to do, she was doing herself, or more accurately she was letting happen what was supposed to happen, without resistance. She was dying, but peacefully, as her messages had told us. Once again, there was a lesson for me here. My job, as has so often been true during my lifetime, was simply to pay attention.

SWIMMING IN
THE ARCHIVES

A ll my life, people have asked me, "What does it feel like to be the daughter of Charles and Anne Lindbergh?" and all my life I haven't known how to answer.

If someone asks what it feels like to be you, what do you say?

I've tried to answer the question politely and honestly, because that's what I was brought up to do. When I was young, I'd say something like, "It's okay, I guess," or words to that effect. This must have been disappointing. The questioners probably hoped to hear something like, "It's very exciting and glamorous," or "It's really historic," or "It's a great privilege."

What would have been closest to the truth is, "It feels completely normal to me. It's the only life I've ever known." Equally true is, "It feels extremely weird, sometimes."

One extremely weird thing is the existence of archives. Most families have attics, not archives. Families like mine, where there are individuals whose lives have held the public's interest for almost a century, have archives. My parents were aviator-explorers and authors with widespread and varied public and private experiences. This means that their archives exist in institutions throughout the country. There is so much material stored in these institutions—libraries, museums, colleges, universities, and historical societies—that it is hard for me to remember who has what. (Imagine trying to find a specific family photograph album, for instance, if there are half-a-dozen family attics, each in a different state.)

Fortunately, where there are archives, there are also archivists. If I want to know how to find something in a Lindbergh archive, anywhere in the country, that's who I contact: the archivists at Yale's Sterling Memorial Library most often, but also at the Sophia Smith Collection at Smith College and the Smithsonian National Air and Space Museum, the Minnesota History Center, the Missouri Historical Society, and occasionally others. When I visit it's like having protective, wise, and extraordinarily courteous native guides to the strange land where my family history meets the history of my country and the world, a place that has been *terra incognita*, at least mostly *incognita*, for much of my life.

I say "mostly" because during the past twenty years I have become more familiar with my family history through my own research and writing, as well as that of others. During my father's lifetime and after his death during my mother's remaining years, researchers and scholars who wanted access to any of the Lindbergh archives needed signed permission from one of my parents or two of their children. After my mother's death in 2001, we found that she had left instructions that for ten more years, such access would still require the signatures of two of her children. Permission should be given by her children, according to her will, "only in instances where they feel that constructive results will be achieved."

That phrase plunged me, headfirst and sputtering, into archival oceans from which I have not yet fully emerged today. I became the family member most involved with the archives after my mother's death, partly because I was named co-executor, with my oldest brother Jon, of my mother's literary estate. (Our sister Anne had originally been a co-executor, but Anne died in 1993, eight years before our mother's passing.) I can stay afloat in these waters, and I pretty much understand where things are. Most of the material on the flight to Paris is at the Missouri Historical Society in St. Louis, for example, while most of my father's boyhood memorabilia and artifacts are in Minnesota. Most of my mother's manuscripts and early diaries and letters are at Smith, while the later ones, along with my father's materials of the same period, are at Yale.

I can make my way when I have to from one place to the other—with the help of the archivists, of course—and I can find what I need . . . most of the time. For a while following my mother's death, I simply followed my mother's example, in consultation with my brothers. Our mother outlived our father by almost three decades and was always very strict about his papers, allowing access primarily to those whose work he had authorized while he was living. She gave almost no access to her own papers at all, and told us that she did not want to authorize a biography of herself while she was still living.

Our father, during his lifetime, had authorized and encouraged a biography of his own father by historian Bruce Larson—*Lindbergh of Minnesota*, published by Harcourt Brace Jovanovich in 1971—as well as a study of his own involvement in the isolationist movement during the period leading up to World War II (*Charles A. Lindbergh and the Struggle Against Intervention in World War II* by Wayne S. Cole, published by Harcourt Brace Jovanovich in 1974). He further authorized and worked closely on what both my father and his friend and publisher William Jovanovich called a "military biography" by military historian Colonel Raymond Fredette, a book which was to cover my father's experiences in and with the US military. This book has never been published, possibly because both my father and Jovanovich died before the author could complete it, but also—or so I believe—because Colonel Fredette always had a deep respect for my mother, and may have discovered things in my father's life that he did not want her to know.

My father worked on his own autobiography toward the end of his life, but it was still unfinished at the time of his death; after extensive work by Jovanovich and Yale archivist Judith Schiff, Harcourt Brace Jovanovich published the manuscript in 1976 as *Autobiography of Values*.

I am not sure why our mother felt so strongly about not authorizing a biography of herself while she was alive. Partly, I think, it had to do with an innate and lifelong self-consciousness, partly with a fear that she might have to spend precious hours being interviewed about her life when she would prefer to spend those hours living it, and partly about her own writing. She had already chronicled her own life extensively, first in her early books about flying with my father, later in her semi-autobiographical novels. Even *Gift from the Sea*, her most famous book, was a kind of philosophical memoir. Finally, she published five volumes of diaries and letters covering the years from 1922, when she was a schoolgirl of sixteen, to the end of the Second World War. All of this, she seemed to think, should suffice.

Several people wrote books about my mother during her lifetime anyway, without access to her archives. Each one of them approached her first with a request to see her private or archived papers, and accepted her refusal with respect. One writer told the family that she wasn't really writing a biography of my mother at all. Instead, the book would be a "story of the Morrow women." Though wary, my mother was willing to meet this writer and talk with her on that basis, though she still refused access to the archives. My mother always had good instincts: when that "Morrow women" book was published a year before my mother's death, it turned out to be essentially a biography of Anne Morrow Lindbergh after all.

In recent years there have been other books about my mother, at least one of them disconcertingly fictional. I feel sure there will be others in the future, but I probably won't read many of them. For me it has always been far more illuminating, and more moving, to read about my mother's life in her own words.

Several years after our mother died, my brother Land and I, along with our niece Kristina Lindbergh and our friend and colleague Carol Hyman, embarked on a project to extend my mother's published diaries and letters beyond the last volume, *War Within and Without*, which came out in 1980 by Harcourt Brace Jovanovich and left the reader in 1944. We spent many days in the Yale archives together, and over three years we amassed more than two thousand pages of my mother's letters and journals from the second half of her life. We worked with Yale archivists to locate, collect, and copy the materials, then Carol's son Andrew deciphered my mother's elegant but often nearly illegible handwriting from carbon copies of diary entries and personal letters, and then he typed these out neatly on the computer. Finally, with the guidance and wisdom of my mother's longtime editor, Altie Karper at Random House, we condensed the mass of material into a manageable book-sized volume covering the years from 1947 to 1986, titled *Against Wind and Tide*, which was published in 2012. It wasn't something my mother had intended to do herself, but I think if she had lived longer, she might have come to it.

Many things changed for my mother as she got older. In 1977, three years after my father's death and during the fiftieth anniversary year of his famous flight from New York to Paris, she gave a television interview to Eric Sevareid of CBS at her home in Connecticut, speaking "about her husband's life and death and about her philosophy," as the online description of the interview tells us. I don't think she had ever done anything like this during my father's lifetime.

After their conversation, Mr. Sevareid sent my mother a small and thriving spruce tree in a pot. She planted it at the edge of the lawn and named it after him. Anyone who didn't know about the interview probably would have been terribly disconcerted when she pointed out a bird flying over the cove, or a view of the islands further out, by saying "Look just to the left of Eric Sevareid," but her family and friends knew exactly what she meant.

She also had an interview for a *Smithsonian World* television series in 1984. The interview aired on PBS as "Crossing the Distance," and the interviewer was writer and historian David McCullough. He won an Emmy Award for the interview, and my mother decided after their conversation that if David McCullough ever asked, she would allow him to write a book about her, and would even give permission for him to use the archives.

Knowing that David McCullough was busy not only writing his own books but also with many other projects, I was not sure that he would be able to take on this one, but I was charmed, and touched, by my mother's response to him, her sense of friendship and trust. I thought of it almost romantically (*She'll only dance with David!*) and it seemed to me that he should know. I wrote to him, and he responded with appreciation, though he was indeed committed to other work at that time. The subject did not come up again, and my mother did not endorse another biographer—not for herself, anyway.

There was one biographer, finally, to whom she gave access to everything: my father's papers at all institutions, her own papers everywhere, as well as a personal letter of approval he could take to her friends and relatives, so that they would speak to him without fear of distressing her.

The biographer was A. Scott Berg, and the proposed biography would be about her husband, not herself, though Berg made it clear at the outset that he felt their marriage was "the heart of the story," as he once said to me. He let us know, too, that he would not attempt a biography without full archival access, as he did not believe that a responsible biography could be written without it. He would need to see everything and talk with everybody, he told my mother, extremely politely, the first time they met. She agreed.

It might have been because, as she said following that first meeting, "He seems to be such a *nice* young man," which statement delighted Berg, at the time approaching forty. Or it is possible that she had read at least some of the two earlier, highly praised biographies he had sent to her: *Maxwell Perkins, Editor of Genius*, and *Goldwyn, A Biography*. I suspect, though, that she simply liked and trusted Scott Berg, as we all did. (David McCullough wrote to me, when the news became public, "Your mother could not have made a better choice.") And besides, when she learned that this biographer planned to allow eight to ten years for the research and writing of the book, she said to me cheerfully, "Oh, that's all right. I'll be dead by then!"

As it turned out, she was still living when the book was published in 1998, and by then Scott Berg had become a family friend. Not only that, but for me he had become a kind of Super-Archivist, such a meticulous researcher that he knew how to find everything Lindbergh-related everywhere. I relied upon him to supply names and dates and places I couldn't remember while I was working on my own 1998 memoir, *Under a Wing*. Even now, long after *Lindbergh, A Biography* won the Pulitzer Prize, I still contact him when I'm looking for something I don't know how to find in the archives.

Recently, I spent a number of days during the heat of summer looking for rights information connected with my father's 1953 book, *The Spirit of St. Louis*. I was doing this on behalf of a composer and music teacher from St. Louis who had written a cantata in 2002, based on an excerpt from the book. At that time, the musical piece was intended for local high school performers and a local audience. Permission to use the excerpt was given without hesitation. Now, however, the composer was being represented by a music publishing company that intended to publish his work commercially. They needed all the appropriate legal permissions.

I don't know much about music rights, except that they are complicated. In fact, all the rights for *The Spirit of St. Louis* are complicated. The book was first published in 1953 by Charles Scribner's Sons, a well respected publishing company later purchased by Simon and Schuster. Did Simon and Schuster have to give permission for the publication of an excerpt from *The Spirit of St. Louis* in a cantata? About fifty years ago, a bank and a major motion picture company also held some of the rights to *The Spirit of St. Louis*. For a brief time before this, my mother had the rights, all of them. My father had given them to her.

No more treading water in the archives for me. I had to dive in deep. In researching my own files at home, I found a 1994 memo from my parents' lawyer, outlining the status of their various copyrights at that time. I learned this about *The Spirit of St. Louis*:

> By agreement dated September 19, 1952, Charles A. Lindbergh transferred the manuscript for this book and all rights of ownership therein to Anne Morrow Lindbergh as Trustee. Mrs. Lindbergh resigned on March 31, 1954 and appointed J. P. Morgan & Co., Incorporated (now Morgan Guaranty Trust Company of New York) as Successor Trustee. Lindbergh retained no rights in this work.

It was now more than two decades after this memo had been written. Did Morgan Guaranty, now JP Morgan Chase, still own the rights and therefore have the obligation to deal with the composer and his publisher? I began to call bankers.

I started with the banker whose name and phone number I found on my New York checking account statement. I rarely use this account, but once or twice a year funds are transferred into it from what we in the family call "*The Spirit of St. Louis* Trust," established at the time the book was sold to Hollywood for the Jimmy Stewart film for the benefit of my father's children and grandchildren.

"Literary rights?" said the very courteous young man with whom I first spoke at JP Morgan Chase. He transferred me to someone else in the trust department, who sent me on to a senior trust officer, who said something very like what the first banker had said. "Literary rights?"

Fortunately, by now I was in touch with my own literary agent, Jennie Dunham, who told me that she would gladly handle the music rights permissions for my family, as soon as we could establish which of these rights the family controlled. What about that film made from the book in the 1950s? Which company had bought the rights, and what rights had they purchased?

Warner Brothers. My research would have to involve Hollywood studios. With this thought I could suddenly hear Darth Vader music (even though the *Star Wars* series came from 20th Century Fox). Did Warner Brothers own the rights to use words from my father's book in a cantata? I dimly recollected a conversation with Scott Berg, who grew up in Hollywood and is still very much involved with the world of film studios and films. I thought he and I had once discussed the film contract for *The Spirit of St. Louis*, and I thought he said it contained language giving Warner Brothers "all rights in any media now existing and any yet to be invented throughout the universe." Something like that.

Where was that contract? Did it still exist? If so, where was it?

I contacted Scott Berg once again with these questions, while at the same time Jennie Dunham was working her own contacts at Scribner/Simon and Schuster and talking with our family's trust officer at JP Morgan Chase. Both organizations were very glad to work with Jennie, though the music company people were increasingly uneasy. Why was this taking so long? It was a "very simple permission," and the first performance of the cantata was scheduled for October. The music company had enjoyed much better cooperation from the representatives of Stephen King, for a musical production of *The Shining*.

I was sorry about that, but I was moving as fast as I could. Swimming in the archives is no dip in some Hollywood pool.

Scott Berg was wonderfully prompt in answering my questions about the Warner Brothers contract. Surprising me, he did not advise seeking what I was looking for in Hollywood. He said instead, "The contract must be in one of those boxes at Yale. I mean, come on. Are you suggesting that C. A. L. might have possibly thrown it out?" This from the man who spent ten years going through seven hundred boxes in the Lindbergh Collection at the Sterling Library at Yale and knew that my father never discarded papers of potential historical interest. My mother, probably intimidated and unsure as to her husband's notion of historical interest, also discarded almost no papers at all, just in case.

I would try Yale, of course, but first I thought I'd look again in my own files. I had seen a film contract recently, I knew I had, while looking for something else. I went upstairs to the room I sometimes call my office, because among the many other things I keep there (old suitcases, boxes of clothes and other items to be given away, some outsized stuffed animals people have given to me that the grandchildren like to drag downstairs to play with), I have several wall-sized file cabinets for old files and records, photographs, and ancient family documents that nobody will ever need again, but what if they do?

I slid open a bulging drawer labeled "Lindbergh and Morrow files," and there it was, a copy of an agreement "made and entered into this 22nd day of July, 1954, between LELAND HAYWARD PRODUCTIONS, Inc. a New York Corporation, and BILLY WILDER Productions, Inc. a California corporation, parties of the first part, and WARNER BROS. PICTURES, Inc. a Delaware corporation, party of the second part . . ." and on it went for sixty-five pages. What a relief!

I sent off a copy of the document to Jennie Dunham in New York, after having looked through it in a cursory fashion. I did find the phrase I remembered, about Warner Brothers having "the sole and exclusive right to distribute, exhibit, advertise, publicize and exploit . . . by any and all media now or hereafter known and in any manner whatsoever . . ." but this phrase, disappointingly, referred only to the planet Earth, not the universe. Too bad. Still, I'd found the contract!

Except that as Jennie Dunham gently informed me after she had received and read carefully every page of the document, it was the wrong contract. We did not need to know about the rights arrangements between Billy Wilder, Leland Hayward, and Warner Brothers as to the photoplay for the film, to which this contract referred. We needed to know which rights (if any) to the actual book, *The Spirit of St. Louis*, had been retained by my family and which rights remained with Scribner and/or had been granted to JP Morgan or, eventually, to Warner Brothers.

Back to the bank.

We were told by the bankers that JP Morgan Chase had "scrubbed the files" (what does *that* mean?) but could not locate the original 1954 agreement for *The Spirit of St. Louis* Trust.

Back to Yale. At this point I called upon Carol Hyman, who had worked with us in the archives during the production of *Against Wind and Tide*. She made a couple of phone calls and did some research online, locating and sending to me an inventory of Yale's Lindbergh Collection. One page clearly identified the location of my parents' business and publishing contracts: Box 354 file 354691, "Business Contracts;" Box 355 file 355701, "Publishing Contracts."

Judy Schiff, the Yale archivist who had edited my father's unfinished autobiography, promised to see to the matter personally. Judy exceeded my expectations and came up with the archival pot of gold. This treasure, from Box 355 file 355701, consisted of 517 beautifully bound pages of trusts and agreements concerning *The Spirit of St. Louis*, inscribed on the flyleaf with these words:

> To Charles Lindbergh
> Marking the end of a long and I hope successful negotiation.
> Yours,
> William Wilder
> November 9, 1954

I'm not completely sure that the date is November 9—it could be November 4—and I'm not sure that the last word of the sentence is "negotiation," though I can't figure out what other word it could be. I found it hard to read Mr. Wilder's handwriting, but my other guesses were improbable: infestation? irrigation? The archivists at Yale kindly scanned and sent the entire manuscript to me, and I printed out all 517 pages. The original manuscript had yellowed a bit over the years, and I had to replace my printer cartridge twice before the job was done, but it was worth it.

I have it now. The whole story. I can answer questions about rights and permission going all the way back to 1952. The documentation is here, all 517 pages of it, thanks to Billy Wilder and the archivists.

I can swim along in the archives with *The Spirit of St. Louis* and have no fear of drowning in documents, swim with grace and confidence and aplomb and fortitude, and—who knows?—if I do this for long enough, maybe someday I'll get to Paris.

THESE TREES

❝ These oaks!" my husband Nat sighed as we drove slowly around the corner and started up the dirt road through the woodlot. His voice held something richer than recognition or admiration: a quality of affectionate awe. He loves these trees, their trunks seventy feet tall on both sides of our path, with the last bright scatterings of leaves far above our heads still golden in the late October light. Each oak leaf, even from this distance, showed its distinctive shape.

In the red oaks, the leaf-points are sharp and delicate, unlike the rounded mitten-like bumps that characterized the white oak leaves on the trees I grew up with in southern Connecticut. There were oaks and other hardwood trees on the land around the house of my childhood on Long Island Sound; later, in the towns in New England where I went to school; and finally, here in Vermont where I have lived as an adult. I've lived on this farm for more than twenty-five years: wife, mother, grandmother, a woman who keeps sheep and chickens, grows flowers.

But it is my husband who is familiar with trees.

There are maple trees as well as oaks on this road, but by late October in northern Vermont the fiery colors of the maples have gone; their leaves are on the ground, their branches bared to the open sky. Now the oaks show themselves unrivalled, standing exactly where they have always stood, and my husband has called them fervently by name.

Nat's days are filled with trees this season. Every morning that he isn't busy with a writing project or a meeting, or thwarted by pouring rain, he goes up to the woodlot with the tools for making firewood: the chainsaw for cutting down carefully selected trees; the ax; a splitting maul and wedges for chopping, cutting, and splitting the logs into smaller sections; and a peavey, my favorite tool in the collection, and one familiar to loggers for a hundred years. When you see those handsome, black-bearded French-Canadian loggers balancing upon huge logs in raging rivers, while deftly turning and directing the logs downstream, the thing they turn the logs with is a peavey.

Most important to Nat, though, is the old Ford tractor, with a winch in back for hauling felled trees out of the woods after his chainsaw has lopped off any branches that might tangle with brush and undergrowth as he drags each log to the clearing. Here, he will turn the log into a pile of split firewood. It won't be this year's firewood, but next year's, and it may even be designated for the year after that. Anyone who cuts firewood knows that it needs a winter or two to age and dry before it is safe to use in the wood stove or the fireplace. Burning green wood too soon after it has been cut creates a dangerous mix of tar and creosote that can coat the chimney and cause a fire. One such chimney fire destroyed my father's first home in Minnesota.

Nat mainly cuts maple for firewood. There are plenty of maple trees here on the farm, and maple burns well. As part of his woodlot management plan, he may harvest an oak tree or two, but not the oaks that border the road to the woodlot. He likes those exactly where they are, and he pays careful attention to them.

A few weeks ago, he noticed that there were acorns scattered on the road beneath one of these oak trees, and that occasionally a car or truck would come along and smash a couple of acorns beneath its tires. At about the same time, he observed that two crows were often in this vicinity. As he watched one day a car came past and destroyed an acorn. Immediately, the crows flew to the spot and gathered pieces of the crushed nut, pre-cracked and ready to eat. This was what the birds had been waiting for.

I have an enhanced appreciation of oak trees now, thanks to Nat. I can see the fallen oak leaves covering the ground like puddles as I walk along our road with the dogs, and when I was in town one day I noticed a large, not-yet-raked-up pool of oak leaves on the lawn of the library. There was a boy about ten years old sitting in the deepest part of the pile, his legs completely covered and his arms flailing in an effort to keep the whirls and swarms and eddies of oak leaves flying above him in the crisp air.

"Great leaves!" I said to him cheerfully in greeting. He didn't answer. I wouldn't have answered either, in his position. What was there to say? He knew these were "great leaves" or he wouldn't have been sitting there, doing what he was doing. He knew he was lucky to have found them before the lawn-rakers and picker-uppers came along to clear them all away.

Was he on his way home from school? It was about the right time of day. Was he supposed to be sitting on the library steps, waiting for a parent to come and collect him? Had he seen the leaves from that perch and found himself unable to resist them? I know the feeling: I still scuff through leaves and crunch my way through iced-over mud puddles when I get the chance.

I love making piles of leaves with my rake, as if sweeping the lawn with a tin-tined broom. I don't do too much of this anymore, because Nat tells me that raking the lawn is unnecessary, that, in fact it's "an anal-retentive Anglo-Saxon obsession," because the leaves are good fertilizer for the lawn, and contrary to popular belief, they don't stop the grass from growing. Still, it's nice to have my garden clear of leaves, and I enjoy picking up big clumps of maple leaves in that gardener's embrace where the rake holds one side of the clump and my arm holds the other side and I smell the wet-earth smell as I take them to the heap of garden miscellany under the big lilac bush on the far side of the driveway. This is the place where weeds and sticks and tired pot-less potted plants go to rest and, I fondly hope, to recycle themselves into further organic usefulness during my lifetime.

The leaves I rake are from two ancient maple trees standing on the lawn between the front door of our house and the smaller of two ponds on the property, not far from the driveway. The maple trees originally bordered a road that went right by the house, an early nineteenth-century path followed by settlers of that time, and an Indian trail before the settlers arrived. Other maples once lined this road too. Nat found several enormous stumps along the same path when he first came to the farm in the early 1970s, and feels sure that those maples must have been planted by the settlers, with our two the last surviving trees in the row.

For decades now, they have been our hammock trees—just the right distance apart from one another for this purpose—and they provide the shade for my "shade garden" by the pond, where hosta and pulmonaria and lily-of-the-valley all thrive. Gnarled and twisted, with massive lower limbs outstretched and available to hang swings from, these are not deep forest maples with straight trunks uninterrupted by branches until close to the top. These are family trees, beloved by our family and by countless families of squirrels and chipmunks who take refuge in the holes and hideaways left by fallen branches or pecked into dead limbs by pileated woodpeckers searching for insects.

These trees are often bright with cedar and Bohemian waxwings in early spring, the birds rising up and settling and flitting back and forth like so many flying golden pears (except that pears don't fly, and they don't leave bird poop on the hood of my car, either, when I absentmindedly park it under one of these maples at the wrong time of year). Nat drew my attention a few years ago to a mother duck, a merganser, who has developed the habit of nesting in a cavity in one of the maple trees, about twenty feet off the ground. She lays her eggs there each spring and sits on them until they hatch. Then, one day in June, all the baby mergansers tumble out of the maple tree nest and down to the ground, one after the other. Impossible though it seems as I watch, they all arrive safely and make their way to the pond just a few yards away. Instantly they are able to swim in a more or less orderly line behind their mother, a dignified and stylish-looking duck with a gray body, a white throat, and a "crested rufous head," as our bird book puts it. She is a graceful swimmer and diver, and within minutes, her babies, those balls of fluff she hatched high up in the maple tree and then pushed out of the nest one by one, are swimming and diving too.

We watch this flotilla of ducklings and their mother enjoying the pond for two or three days. They swim, they dive, they play follow-the-leader, they settle down at night on the opposite shore in a sandy area beneath the overhanging grasses of the bank above them. Then, all at once, they're gone. They don't fly away, and they don't swim away: they *walk*, over the fields to the river. I can't imagine how long this takes them, because the river they're walking to is the Passumpsic, at least a mile away and across Vermont Route 5. The trek requires a walk uphill through our hayfields to the top of our land, then down the other side of the hill through woods thick with brush and brambles. While working on fencing in our highest pasture in June, Nat has seen the merganser family on its way from our pond to the river, with the mother quacking encouragement all the way. *Come along, Number One, and leave that grasshopper alone! Number Three, you can do it, just put one little webbed foot in front of the other. Number Seven, I know you're hungry, but the sooner we get there the sooner we can eat . . .*

I hate to think of them all crossing Route 5, where the logging trucks come thundering along every day. I can't believe that even one of the babies will make it all the way to the river. And yet, every fall, a few young mergansers settle briefly on the little pond behind the maple trees—perhaps a nostalgic visit to their birthplace, who knows? And every spring, a female merganser makes her nest in the maple tree, about twenty feet above the ground.

Nat harvests an apple tree on a very small island in the middle of the pond where the baby mergansers learn to swim and dive. To pick the apples in the fall, he puts a canoe in the pond and turns it sideways so that it makes a bridge between the mainland of the lawn and Apple Island, as we have named it. The canoe is full of bushel baskets. Nat makes his way carefully between the baskets and across the canoe-bridge to the island, taking one of the baskets with him. Then, he begins to pick, replacing each empty basket in the canoe with a full one. When all the baskets are full of apples, he steps back across the canoe even more carefully, hoping the boat doesn't sink under the weight of the fruit. When he is on land again, he then pulls the canoe and its harvest to shore.

In spring, the Apple Island tree is white with blossoms, and on the grassy ground somewhere between the trunk of the tree and the edge of the pond there is another duck, a female mallard, who has her own nest and hatches her own ducklings in her own quiet way. She is well hidden from predators and almost impossible for us to see, however hard we are looking for her. I only know she's there because the father duck is nearby, too, with his bottle-green head and sleek body, swimming in the pond by day and sleeping on the shore of Apple Island at night. When the eggs hatch, the whole mallard family moves on to wherever it needs to go.

Like the mergansers, the mallards come back each year, returning to the protection of Apple Island as the merganser family returns to their maple tree. We never see much of the father merganser, a striking black-and-white fellow who shows up with the female in the spring, swims around for a while, then disappears at just about the time his mate heads for her nest in the tree. I don't know where he goes or why, but if I were a mother merganser, I think I'd nudge my daughters in the direction of those nice mallard boys over on Apple Island.

Our woods are full of individual giants, most of them white pines, some of them hemlock or balsam, but to me as I sat looking at them from my chair at the window, for a long time they were undifferentiated, a Great Wall of Forest. As I sat for longer periods, and looked not *at* the forest trees but *into* them, the view began to change and deepen. I began to see the lift of upward curving branches, lighter on the top and rich with rounded darkness underneath. I saw the way these trees fit beside, in front of, and behind one another, sharing soil and sunlight. Where I once saw a wall of trees and called it "woods," now I see shape and movement and the slow dance of living and growing that I mistook for stillness. I learned that when I was impatient or distracted in my watching, I couldn't see.

Like the oaks, the white pines that make up much of our forest have lived on this land for many multiples of my own time here. They have been used to build homes and barns and sheds for generations of humans and animals. The house was built around 1840, a modest New England cape that has sheltered many families and has experienced many changes, including an addition my husband built in 1980, doubling the size of the house to hold a growing family.

The floor on which my chair sits as I write has been here since the house was first built. The trees from which the floor was made were growing in the woods here for two hundred years or more before they were cut for floorboards. The boards are a foot wide, more or less, and they have been sanded and finished and swept and mopped over and over again for about one hundred and seventy-five years. Nat pointed out to me that the width of the boards varies substantially, not only from board to board but from one end of each individual plank to the other end. Nineteenth-century woodsmen did not cut boards in standard widths, as we do today. Instead they cut according to the tapering shape of the felled tree, or as Nat calls it, the "Mother Tree," thinner at the top and wider at the bottom, so that none of the wood is wasted. The board under my chair by the window measures nine inches, but at the other side of the room the same board is ten and a half inches wide. The Mother Tree for this board is a white pine, one that has been on this land in one form or another for almost four hundred years.

"Come out and look at some lumber," Nat said to me in late fall. I went out to the driveway and looked at a pile of boards in the back of his pickup truck. Nat pulled out one board and showed it to me, pointing out the warm, almost rosy color and the pattern made by the annual growth rings. What I saw looked like the watery background in a Japanese print, a representation of liquid moving outward in ripples across the surface of the wood. All this picture needed was a little tree rendered in a few deft strokes of ink, or maybe a long-legged wading crane.

"What is it?" I asked, fascinated.

"It's cherry," he told me. He explained that these boards came from a deep forest cherry tree he had cut down in our woods years ago. This was a huge tree, like one of the white pines, not like the small and twisting cherry trees of our roadsides and pastures. The cherry logs he had cut had sat for some months in the place where they'd fallen, then they had been taken to a small sawmill operation run by a friend in another town. They came back as boards so beautifully sawn that we marveled at each piece, and Nat brought one into the living room to look at and think about. He has special plans for this cherry wood, talking about it in terms of wainscoting or cabinet making.

When my children were very young and I was trying to learn the difference between certain softwoods—pine, balsam, spruce, hemlock—I used to wander around the property, mumbling their names to myself. Finally, my three-year-old daughter protested, "Mommy! Don't talk spruce!" So I stopped.

But today, again, I want to learn the character of the trees, even though I know that the names—at least, the names given to them by humans—are not names the trees themselves use. They speak with bark and branch and leaf, with alterations in shade and sunlight, with the patterns of growth rings and with the activity of birds and animals, with movement inside stillness. Even if these aren't their true names, it is good to speak the designations, even just in my mind, as I watch them and honor them: these apple and cherry orchards of farm and pasture, these maples at the edge of the road and in the woods, the white pines and fir and spruce in the forest, willows by the pond, these birches and beeches, these oaks.

REMNANTS AND
RECIPES

My mother died in 2001, but I'm still finding things in my house that belonged to her. These are not directly inherited items, like furniture or china, or even personal keepsakes, like photographs of her or her letters to me. The things I'm finding don't belong in the category of "memorabilia," either, with the artifacts and papers that my parents donated during their lifetimes to a range of institutions from the Missouri History Center in St. Louis to the Smith College Library. I suppose that some of these things might be appropriate for a historical collection, but the historical collection can't have them. They're mine.

What I keep are mundane and familiar belongings, things she used every day.

I have an overstuffed file drawer where I keep my stationery supplies, staples, boxes of checks, extra packages of my favorite pens, and a bottle of Elmer's glue that I like to have on hand in case I suddenly want to glue something. The Elmer's bottle barely fits in the drawer, jammed in as it is on top of everything else, and I was uneasily aware every time I opened the drawer that I risked a catastrophic sticky mess, so I finally decided to rearrange everything in the drawer. While trying to make more room for the glue bottle, I found and removed my mother's purse—a worn, red leather change purse with a brass snap closure, packed full of long-expired credit cards and other necessities. I had saved it and stashed it between the Elmer's glue and a box of glittery markers I like to hide from small children and dogs. Then I forgot all about it.

I remember now that I couldn't bear to throw the purse away when she died, despite the fact that at the instant of my mother's death everything in it became obsolete.

Not only that, but even at the beginning of the time she came to live in the little house on our farm with round-the-clock caregivers, the house where she eventually died, my mother was well over ninety, mentally fragile, and had not been driving or shopping by herself for years. The driver's license and the credit cards were out of date even then.

Still, for me, the red purse was a comforting kind of time capsule, and I went through it eagerly when I found it again, though with a twinge of uneasiness—Was I being morbid?—as well as a touch of the same guilt I would have felt back in my teens had I been going through my mother's purse without her permission.

My mother, like many other women who lived in the suburbs of New York City in the middle of the last century, had individual credit cards for Bergdorf Goodman, Elizabeth Arden, and B. Altman. Tucked in among those was a tiny metal rectangle housed in a red plastic case. It was a "Charga-Plate," with her name and address embossed. The piece of paper in the case with it indicated that the plate could be used at Bloomingdale's, Franklin Simon, Gimbel Brothers, and Saks Fifth Avenue.

Behind all the charge cards, and the Charga-Plate, I found a many-times-folded piece of my mother's own light blue airmail paper, upon which she had carefully written down all the numbers of all the credit cards she owned, including an Esso gasoline card that was not among those I had seen in the purse. At the bottom of this page she had written, confusingly, "Do not carry this with me."

There are membership cards here too, for the Connecticut Motor Club, the National and the Connecticut Audubon Societies, the Museum of Modern Art, the Metropolitan Museum of Art, the Smithsonian Museum, and the Smith College Museum of Art. There is a Pan Am World Pass in my father's name and a National Aviation

Hall of Fame Life Membership in hers. There is an AARP card and one for Blue Cross Blue Shield of Connecticut. Finally, there is a dog-eared but neatly filled in identification card with her name and address filled in at the top, and mine below. (*IN CASE OF EMERGENCY PLEASE CONTACT . . .*)

This last card of all, I found to my surprise, was one issued by the Euthanasia Education Council, of 250 West 57th Street, New York City (just around the corner from Saks Fifth Avenue!). On the back these words are printed:

> TO MY FAMILY, MY PHYSICIAN, AND ANY HOSPITAL:
>
> If there is no reasonable expectation of my recovery from mental or physical disability . . . I request that I be allowed to die and not be kept alive by artificial means and heroic measures. I ask that medication be mercifully administered to me for terminal suffering even if it hastens the moment of my death.
>
> I hope that you who care for me will feel morally bound to act in accordance with this urgent request.

Her signature at the bottom of the card reads, neatly, "Anne M. Lindbergh."

I had never seen this card before. In the late 1990s, when my mother came to live with us on the farm, we kept on hand an informal, rather vague living will she had signed more than two decades earlier in Connecticut, but nobody ever thought of looking in the red purse for another one.

What would I have thought, had I read the Euthanasia Education Council's handy, purse-sized directive in those final days and months of her life? How would I have interpreted the reference to "mental or physical disability?" For most of the ten years before she died at ninety-four it was very clear that there was no "reasonable expectation" of my mother's recovery from the dementia that left her in daily confusion as to her place in space and time. However, her body and her physical will both remained relatively strong. How could we possibly have obeyed her written request, "let me die," even if we'd known about it? You don't kill somebody because of mental confusion.

I wonder whether a person making a living will or issuing a final directive while fairly healthy can really comprehend how hard it is to carry out their wishes when the time comes for them to begin dying. My sister, who died of cancer, made a living will too, as my mother did, but when Anne was actually dying, the only thing her husband and children and the rest of us felt we could do to help was to allow her as much morphine as possible for pain and to continue to let her have liquid intravenously for sustenance. We could not bring ourselves to deny her water, though not giving her water probably would have hastened the dying process. To do such a thing was unthinkable, when she appeared both to want and to need liquid, moment by moment.

In my mother's case, things were simpler at the actual end of her life than they were for my sister. My mother stopped eating, she slept a great deal, and then she died. We did not know during her last years that she had left in the red purse the Euthanasia Education Council's statement about "mental or physical disability," and she may have forgotten about it herself after she'd signed it. I am glad that I did not discover it until all those years after her very natural death.

Another of my late mother's belongings that I keep is a kind of cookbook she had in the form of a 3½ x 5½-inch black loose-leaf notebook, stuffed to overflowing with recipes cut out from magazines and newspapers for forty years or more. My mother believed, erroneously, that she could not cook, or keep house, or do much of anything in the traditional female world of her day. In the spring of 1947, she wrote in her diary about her failings as a housewife:

> The difficulties lie for me, curiously enough, in what is most ordinary for all the other women in the world—in keeping house, in shopping and cooking, in ordinary living. I am very stupid at it because I have really never done it. I have never shopped and cooked and cleaned for my husband like an ordinary woman.
>
> When most women learn this—when they are first married—I was learning to fly and to navigate and fly a glider. So I do not know a good cut of meat from a poor

one or what things cost by the pound . . . or how to cook
a good steak or omelet.[6]

Here my mother manages to disparage one set of her skills—in
the household—and to toss off dismissively another set—the abilities
that earned her the first woman's glider pilot's license in the United
States, the National Geographic's Hubbard Medal for exploration,
and, for *North to the Orient*, her book describing her exploratory
flights, a National Book Award. Still, she thought of herself as a person who could barely keep house, and could not cook at all.

Whatever she did cook she attributed to somebody else's recipe.
Most of the recipes I have found in the cooking notebook, even the
ones in her own handwriting, have other peoples' names on them:
"Barbie's Pot Roast" from my first sister-in-law, Barbara Robbins;
"Jim Robbins's Hamburgers," from Barbara's father, a former Alaskan
bush pilot; "Ansy's Rognon's au Madere," from my sister, Anne, who
lived for many years in Paris. There is a Craig Claiborne menu from
the *New York Times*, January 4, 1959, for Beef Sukiyaki, which the
chef primly describes as "a beef and vegetable dish of Japanese ori-
gin." There is a "Household Menu for Thursday" ("Frittata Italiana,
Buttered Lima Beans, Stewed Tomatoes, Lemon Sherbet with Crème
de Menthe") from another issue of the *Times*, with a news item on the
reverse side stating that Sir Winston Churchill sent warmest wishes to
President Kennedy, commending Kennedy's reaffirmation of his faith
in the Atlantic Charter, "which Sir Winston had signed twenty years
earlier with President Franklin D. Roosevelt." (I later determined that
this had to be from August 1961).

I'm not sure of the date for "Quick Chicken Gourmet Recipe of
the Month," something called "Chicken Finale" (doesn't that mean
"Terminal Chicken?") but because the recipe relies heavily on canned
soup ("1 cup cooked chicken, diced, 2 cups spaghetti, 1 T butter, 2 T
green pepper, chopped, 1 can condensed cream of chicken soup") I
would put it in the late 1950s, along with a twice-folded glossy paper
rectangle which turned out to be a triptych of casserole recipes from
a women's magazine: "Beef Casserole," "Chicken Casserole," "Tuna
Casserole," made with Campbell's tomato soup, Campbell's cream of
chicken soup, and Campbell's cream of celery soup, respectively. The

1950s were very big on casseroles made with Campbell's soup. I think I remember that people sprinkled Kellogg's cornflakes on top of the casseroles, but maybe I'm making that up.

When I read all of this, I am quite confused, because my mother didn't cook with Campbell's soup and cornflakes. She really didn't. And another thing puzzles me. I looked through all the clipped recipes that were spilling out of the little black notebook, and I didn't recognize any of them as hers. "Link Sausages with White Wine"— are you kidding? "Potluck Casserole with Kidney Beans, Elbow Macaroni, Ground Beef and Chili Powder"? I don't think so. "Souper Baked Chicken" with Swanson's frozen chicken parts and cream of chicken soup? It just didn't ring a bell.

Where, I thought, were the ingredients so dear to my mother's culinary heart? Where was the tarragon? Where were the mushroom and the little bits of bacon? Where were the chicken livers? Where was the *sherry*, for heaven's sake? It became clear to me that if I wanted to rediscover my mother's cuisine as I knew it, I had to dig deeper.

Under all the piles of clipped recipes, I found something in her handwriting, in French: *Rognons de veau en casserole*. When I searched the phrase online, the first hit was from food writer Tom McNamee, who'd sampled our old friend Craig Claiborne's recipe and had a glowing, if somewhat unexpected, take on it:

> *They do not taste like pee.* Veal kidneys with mustard sauce are one of the great classics of French cooking for a reason: The dish is fantastic.[6]

We were a long way from 1959 and beef sukiyaki. A bit startled, I went back to my mother's cookbook, and found another magazine recipe for veal kidneys, this time in plain English: "Veal Kidney Casserole," with one-half pound of sliced mushrooms, three slices of French bread, some Parmesan cheese, and a quarter cup of sherry. That was more like it.

I don't actually remember my mother cooking "rognons de veau," but these recipes may have been recorded or clipped at a time in my life when I wouldn't have eaten veal kidneys if my very survival had depended upon it. In the late 1950s and early 1960s I was in my teens. Not a chance.

When I about twenty, I lived in Paris for a year and learned to cook chicken livers from one of my mother's recipes. She called it "chicken livers with bacon" (and flour, and sherry), and it was delicious. It turned up in the notebook as a clipping from a French magazine: "Foies de Volaille Marianne" ("Marianne," a beautiful woman with ribbons in her hair and a patriotic expression, has been the emblem of the French Republic since 1792), in which red wine and shallots and consommé and mushrooms accompany the bacon and the "foies," or livers.

Looking for more familiar menus, I continued to time-travel through the fluttering piles of clipped recipes and into the heart of the notebook, where my mother had written down some other French-sounding recipes: "Quick Beef Bourguignon," with red wine and mushrooms but also, surprisingly, "two cans of beef stew." The canned beef stew, like so many things in my family's life, I chose to blame on my father. Canned beef stew was definitely his style, not hers.

When her husband was home, or when any of her sons or sons-in-law came to stay, my mother went to the grocery store and bought Meat: sirloin steaks, pork or lamb chops, sometimes hamburger, which she mixed up in a bowl with parsley and onion and a fresh egg to hold the whole thing together before it turned into patties. Men, she thought, should have Meat. They were entitled to it, they thrived on it, they *deserved* it, because they were Men. If she was alone, or if Anne or I or her own sister or sister-in-law was visiting, we would have lady-dinners, with chicken and salad and a glass of wine, or just a light, delightful cheese omelet, which, despite her self-deprecation, would be perfectly cooked and tasted somehow European. We were different, we Women, subtler than Men and nourished on quieter, less carnivorous foods. Men needed Meat, and they got it.

I loved rediscovering her recipe for "Petits Pois Paysanne," or peasant-style baby peas, with onions and bacon. "Don't overcook!" she warns. It's hard to force yourself to eat overcooked peas, I know. I remember those from my childhood, not cooked by my mother, but by Martha, a German cook who lived with us. She made delicious cookies and very boring vegetables. The overcooked peas would get stuffed into cracks and crannies of the dining room table, or slipped into napkins or hidden under the silverware, but my mother's peas, ambrosial, would melt in the mouth.

And there in the notebook was her "Croque Monsieur" too. This is really just toast with ham and Swiss cheese, but as I remember my mother dipped the toast in egg and sautéed it in butter and served it "with a beautiful cream sauce made of thick cream, butter, very little flour and some of the grated Swiss cheese."

There was a recipe for fondue, written entirely in French and asking for "150 grammes" of Emmenthal cheese and the same of Gruyère, as well as a "decilitre of "vin blanc de Neuchâtel," white wine from an area in Switzerland not far from Les Monts-de-Corsier, the little village where my mother spent thirty summers later in her life. She lived in a chalet my father designed and had built on a hillside above the town of Vevey. She had a magnificent view of the lake known as "Lac Léman" to the Swiss, but it is still called "Lake Geneva" by many English-speaking visitors.

Between deciphering my mother's familiar but not always legible handwriting and translating from a foreign language, I didn't understand everything I was reading, but I was able to discover that in creating this Swiss fondue, she used a "caquelon," a traditional Swiss earthenware cooking dish, with a wooden spoon and a *lot* of kirsch. And very tasty it was, with cut up pieces of French baguettes we speared and then dipped into the cheese/wine/kirsch mixture with those long, thin fondue forks that aren't much good for anything else, accompanied by several glasses of whatever was left of that vin de Neuchâtel. There was never any leftover kirsch, more's the pity.

Straight across the lake from where we ate our meals, you could see the French Alps, and to the east the valley of the Rhone River, with the Swiss Alps at the far end of the valley and the Rhone Glacier at the foot of the peaks. My father loved the Rhone Glacier, as he did so many of the more extreme elements in the universe: floods, earthquakes, elephants, whales, stars. I remember annual excursions to the Rhone Glacier when I was a teenager, slumped sulkily in the back of my parents' Volkswagen, finally climbing out when we'd arrived at that thick blue mass, an expanse of ice and snow that was, inevitably, dull and grubby-looking on the surface. In my opinion at the time, old snow was old snow, wherever you found it. The glacier was as still and solid and dully incomprehensible to me as the great inert tongues of hardened lava that my father took me to see years later in Hawaii.

But I liked the daydreaming possibilities afforded by the long, quiet drive home to the chalet where my mother waited for us, and I loved the meals she gave us when we returned.

Many of these meals are not included in the recipe notebook, though I've searched for them. I can't find "Filets de Perche," which was my husband's favorite among my mother's Swiss meals. Maybe "fried perch" seemed too simple and obvious for her to write down, but these were exquisitely flavored morsels of perch, bought at the farmer's market and probably caught that very day in a small nearby pond or "étang," served with lemon, a green salad, and parsley-flavored new potatoes.

But toward the end of the notebook, to my surprise and joy, I found a recipe that I remember from my mother's Connecticut life: "Mrs. Swan's Chicken and Sherry." "Mrs. Swan" is an abbreviation for Mrs. Swanson (no relation to the Swanson of frozen potpies). She was a short, sturdy, smiling Swedish woman who lived locally with her husband and their niece, Ingrid, and came in by day to work for my parents as a cook/housekeeper in the 1960s and 1970s. Mrs. Swanson called my mother "Mrs. Lindbergh," in a high and lilting Scandinavian voice, but referred to my father, who had become a Brigadier General in the Air Force Reserve under President Eisenhower, as "the Yeneral" or "Yeneral Lindbergh."

After my father's death in 1974, Mrs. Swanson continued to work for my mother until her own retirement, and often prepared a meal that my mother could heat up after she left at the end of the day. A teetotaler by habit, Mrs. Swanson nonetheless used sherry in this recipe. She made allowances for my mother because, as she said once, "Mrs. Lindbergh has lived in Europe," apparently forgetting that she herself had lived in Europe too.

It looks to me as though my mother wrote this recipe down hastily, perhaps while spying on Mrs. Swanson and pretending not to, or by asking casual questions in the kitchen. I don't think Mrs. Swanson ever wrote her recipes down. My husband is the same kind of cook, and you have to snatch culinary information from these people as you can. This is what my mother wrote:

Mrs. Swan's Chicken and Sherry

Dry well in paper towels
Salt & powder with flour
Brown in butter (or oil)
Put in baking dish & cover with broth
Put in 350 degree oven for one hour or more, basting
frequently

Basting Liquid:
1 Cup of chicken broth
1 Cup of sherry
Thicken with flour and more broth & sherry if necessary

That's it. I don't remember whether she covered this dish with a lid or aluminum foil while it was baking (I think she did, for the first half hour or so), and I don't know if she used only certain chicken pieces, but I think I remember little drumsticks and dainty thighs, the smaller, more ladylike parts, not the two-inch-thick breasts or those boneless flat strips that could come from almost anywhere on the bird.

Mrs. Swan's Chicken and Sherry was a delicacy to be savored and remembered, as I am remembering it now. I've been thinking about it, in fact, ever since I found the recipe. Pretty soon I'm going to try it. Though my husband loves to cook and usually makes our evening meals, I'm going to go out and find some ladylike chicken parts, and some sherry, and some flour and some chicken broth, and I'm going to cook this for us the way Mrs. Swanson used to cook it for my mother and the Yeneral. Maybe I'll broil some tomatoes, too, with bread crumbs and tarragon and a drop of olive oil. My mother liked those. I might make a salad with watercress and endives and Boston lettuce and chopped tomatoes, and dress it with my mother's salad dressing, also not written down. She kept all the ingredients for salad dressing together on a wooden tray in one of the cupboards: olive oil, red wine vinegar (I don't think they used balsamic vinegar so much in those days), dry mustard, salt and pepper, basil or tarragon, a little sugar in a bowl. The dry mustard was kept in a small ceramic pot the color of a ripe blueberry, and there was a larger china bowl on the tray for mixing it all together. The salad always tasted the same—a little tangy because of the mustard, gentled by the sugar—perfect.

I suppose I'd better add something of my own, maybe bread. I love to make bread, and a nice crusty baguette would be good with this meal. Salad, French bread, Chicken and Sherry. It sounds delicious.

There is only one problem with all of this. Even if I follow my mother's written instructions to the letter and create this meal exactly as I know she did, I will be aware that there is something—or, rather, someone—missing, and that her absence will make all the difference in the quality of the meal. For that reason, as every daughter knows, no matter how carefully I prepare it, my mother's "Mrs. Swan's Chicken and Sherry" won't ever taste quite as good as I remember.

COLLECTIONS

After Phoebe went to bug camp, I began to look at butterflies in a whole new way. I even started paying attention to caterpillars and spiders, which I had previously more or less ignored, beyond occasionally admiring a dew-spangled spider web on an early morning, or stopping to gaze at a particularly striking set of caterpillar segments undulating through the grass.

It's not easy to ignore these creatures entirely, as they crawl along in my garden or fly above us in the hayfields or dangle at the outer edges of webs they have constructed in the corners of the porch ceiling. I notice these every time I go in and out of the kitchen door.

I don't mind the spiders on my porch because, like the swallows nesting under the eaves of our old farmhouse, they eat flies. (I do mind flies.) I like the caterpillars, too, except the tent caterpillars that strip leaves off trees all over New England and have to be controlled by dubious chemicals. And I love butterflies, but I love them absent-mindedly, appreciating that they are beautiful but not feeling the need to do anything about their beauty except to be grateful for it. I don't seek intimacy with insects.

Phoebe does. Up close and personal is where she likes to be when it comes to creeping, crawling, and fluttering things. She finds them, captures them very gently, and puts them in jars or in cardboard containers, or, in the case of the butterflies, in a specially designed collapsible fine-mesh butterfly cage, about the size and shape of an old-fashioned beer keg. She studies the captive butterflies for a while, looking at them carefully through the gauzy walls of their temporary home, observing their markings and the shapes of their wings, peering at them from every angle, right side up and upside down and sideways. When she's finished looking, whether for an hour or an afternoon, she opens the cage door wide and lets them go.

That's what has made me look at butterflies differently. Thanks to Phoebe they have been, very briefly, visitors in my life from another world. I can take a good look, confirm in a guide whether they are Monarchs or Admirals or Sulfurs or Fritillaries or Painted Ladies, marvel at the intricate details of their existence—the patterns on their wings, the delicate structure of their tiny bodies—and then they're gone again into the air, where they belong. They are not sheep or chickens or household pets. They do not form part of any collection for which I am responsible except, in the lightest possible way, the collection of memory.

During the same summer that Phoebe and I were looking at butterflies, my husband was disposing of his mother's—Phoebe's great-grandmother's—earthly goods. She had died the preceding winter at the age of ninety-six. In nine-and-a-half decades, a person can accumulate a great many earthly goods, and my mother-in-law, a woman of character, charm, fine taste, and a certain ferocity, definitely did.

Generally, my mother-in-law and I got along very well. She reminded me of the women in my own mother's family, New England ladies with old-fashioned good manners and a particular inner sparkle. She was very fond of my two daughters. We were fond of her in return, and we enjoyed her company over the years. But we agreed that she was too often thoughtlessly unkind and, occasionally, really cruel to Nat.

I'm not even sure that Alice realized how often she criticized him for some perceived fault or accused him of "neglecting her," whether by not visiting her as often as she wished or by not paying proper attention to her when they were together. Her anger toward him at times stunned and distressed me. I confronted her about it once when she visited us, but this only caused a flood of tears and the demand that Nat drive her back to her home—three hours away from our farm—immediately. She was so upset that he made the six-hour round trip that day and came home exhausted.

Although she did not show the signs of dementia or other cognitive difficulties that can result in unexplained bursts of anger, these episodes with Nat seemed to increase toward the end of her life. At my daughter's wedding, she poked him—hard!—in the back with her cane. She said this was because he "had not brought her any food," though I had heard her refuse a full plate earlier when he offered it.

There she was, a small, well-dressed woman in her nineties with beautiful white hair, attacking her six-foot son with her cane. It happened very fast, nobody was really hurt, and we who were close to the scene were able to laugh about it later, but we were also appalled: it was so *mean*.

Nat always told me he was "used to" his mother. I never heard him speak to her discourteously or complain about her to those who loved her, and I suspect that most people she knew never saw her behave the way she did at Lizzy's wedding.

Before her death, Alice had lived alone for more than twenty-five years in a large, historic, un-insulated Colonial home in a small New England village. The house was full of rooms, and the rooms were full of things: solid maple beds and rickety night stands, standing lamps and threadbare Oriental rugs, deep blanket chests, big-bosomed bureaus with lace bureau scarves on top, sofas and side chairs and books and paintings, and a grand piano. With several staircases, fireplaces in many of the bedrooms, an attic and a vast, dark basement, the house was a delight to visiting children and a challenge to maintain. Alice had purchased the place because she loved it, and she remained in residence there until the last day of her life in the company of a battalion of belongings.

Some of these had been in the family for many generations. Alice knew their provenance by heart: who they had originally belonged to, where they had come from, and—in some cases, the greatest mystery of all—what they were for. My mother-in-law's comprehensive understanding of her silver alone, her knives and forks and spoons and other items for the dining room, was an education. Nobody could lay out a place setting at a Thanksgiving table more quickly or more accurately, with dinner knives, salad forks, soup and dessert spoons all in their proper positions.

Her silver came from many families down through the years, much of it engraved with initials only she could decipher: *E.A.L, A.F.L, E.D.L, A.T.P.* The flatware reposed in velvet-lined compartmented cases of gleaming wood, mahogany or cherry, created just for this purpose. After her death, though, my husband found some of the flatware had migrated in very small packages to other places in her home, squirreled away as if for a series of tiny, improbable formal meals. These packets were sometimes wrapped in tissue paper, sometimes simply piled together in unlikely combinations and tucked into a coat pocket or a shoebox at the back of her closet, or at the bottom of a deep blanket chest: three teaspoons, four butter knives, and a fish fork. There were also bundles of cash, folded bills stuffed here and there, perhaps to foil burglars, perhaps for emergencies. Thinking about what a true emergency might be for a small elderly woman in a big house with unpredictable plumbing and heating, I can imagine several that might require cash, but as yet none that would call for a silver fish fork.

When it came time to make an inventory of everything she owned following her death, the enumerated items quickly grew into a quantity that my husband, her only child and legal heir, found overwhelming. At first he wasn't sure what to do with it all.

We planned a gathering at her home and invited friends and relatives. Elaine, Alice's part-time housekeeper—lately her more-than-part-time caregiver, though neither woman used the word—cleaned the whole house and had the piano tuned. People came together on the appointed day and told each other stories about Alice, then assembled in the living room to sing her favorite hymn, "Where E'er You Walk," with words by Congreve and music by Handel. Andrea, Alice's niece and my husband's cousin, accompanied the singing on the piano. Alice had told us many times that she wanted this hymn sung at her funeral, and I had written her wish down in my address book, next to her name. I'd also recorded, in tiny letters in the margin of the same crowded page, the other request for her funeral: Ben and Jerry's Coffee Heath Bar Crunch ice cream. Because Alice would have enjoyed it, we served champagne.

There were a few tears as we talked to one another about Alice, and quite a lot of laughter as we listened to the stories we had not heard before. Finally, after everyone but the family members had left, my husband passed out pencils and pieces of paper and asked his relatives to go through the house and put their names on any of the possessions they would like to take home. He had already packed up and distributed among the family much of the silver—several full sets of tableware—and he had chosen and brought to our home in Vermont certain things that he loved, among them a "grandmother" clock, a petite, gentle-voiced version of the classic grandfather clock, and once the property of his own grandmother, Alice's mother. He lived with his mother and his grandmother, both of them divorced during his childhood, and was the only male in the household. He had repaired this clock himself when he was sixteen. It now stands in a corner of our living room, reminding us of the hours and the half-hours with a timid, self-deprecating chime. *Excuse me, it is exactly twelve-o-clock noon.*

My husband brought home some paintings, too, done by his great-uncle, James Wardwell, who had been a post-impressionist landscape artist in New York in the 1920s. With Nat's encouragement, I took a bountiful array of Alice's tasteful scarves and exuberant costume jewelry to share with daughters and granddaughters and women friends. We also took an elegant gold-rimmed bone china set, which sits today on a shelf in our farmhouse pantry, looking as uncomfortable next to our ordinary plates, cups, and glasses as a thoroughbred sharing a stall with sheep.

Most of his mother's belongings, like that clock, had almost certainly come directly from his grandmother's house, where Alice had lived until the grandmother's death in 1980. Alice was one of five daughters, and Nat suspected that his mother may have come away with more than her fair share of the family inheritance, but perhaps because she was the daughter who had been with his grandmother for the last years of her life, the others did not complain.

Alice's one surviving sister, a benign and drifting woman who also had wonderful white hair and bright blue eyes, was well into her nineties at the time of Alice's death, and had no clear recollection as to property divisions in the family. She was shocked to learn of Alice's passing, however, and lamented to her daughter, "But she was so young!"

Nat sent this aunt an emerald ring, the one Alice once said had belonged to the mistress of Napoleon III. He sent to a beautiful poet cousin another ring, a sapphire surrounded by tiny diamonds, given to Alice in her youth, the story went, by the mother of a young man she had refused to marry. This was one of Alice's many romantic narratives, and it fascinated me because I could not make sense of it. Why would any mother do such a thing at such a time? Was the gift a kind of bribe? *Don't marry my son, and I'll give you a ring set with sapphires and diamonds.* Was it a token of gratitude? *Thank God, you won't marry my son!* Or was it, as Alice told us, an act of love? *You will not, alas, become a member of my family, and I am devastated, but please let me give you this ring as a symbol of my undying affection.*

It was a mystery to me, and yet Alice wore the ring every day of her life during the twenty-five years that I knew her. The ring was real, a large and twinkling talisman on her finger, and the story was told over and over again. Combined, the ring and the story were another of her treasures.

Some of the family members were hesitant to go through her house and lay claim to any of her possessions. Others had been in touch with my husband beforehand and understood what was on his mind and his conscience. Andrea, the musical niece who had played Alice's hymn, was delighted that arrangements were being made to ship the grand piano to her home in Portland, Maine. Andrea lived with her husband and children, and cared for her mother, Nat's Aunt Augustine, who got Alice's Napoleonic ring.

By this time in their lives, many of the cousins had children and grandchildren who needed beds and tables and chairs in their houses or apartments. They soon overcame their hesitation and took away any useful pieces of furniture. Some people remembered drawings and paintings and books from their shared grandmother's home, a few were interested in rugs and carpets, and one sweet-natured, mildly autistic cousin piled up photographs in which his own mother appeared, along with several dozen of Alice's unframed watercolor sketches, and took them all away with him.

Beyond collecting things, Alice loved to paint seascapes and sunsets, scenes from Maine and from Vermont, peaceful subjects in pastel colors, and sometimes pen-and-ink sketches of bare trees. These were my favorites. She sat in our kitchen for many hours in winter, once, and sketched the two ancient maples at the edge of our lawn, dark snow-laden limbs reaching out in silence, dry grass on the ground below and dark forest in the distance. With her permission, we had the sketch made into postcards, which we still send out to people who knew Alice, and to people who like trees.

Among all the things hanging on the walls of the big house, there were several I had not noticed before that last day, including two small, framed butterfly collections. When I first saw them, I was inclined to look away, since the whole process of classic butterfly collecting has never appealed to me: the chloroform, the pins, all the weird paraphernalia of lepidopterists. My husband explained to me that these were actually paintings of butterflies arranged to look like mounted collections. The artist was Walter Gifford, another of Alice's uncles and a great admirer of the species, but a man, she claimed, who was too tenderhearted to kill butterflies. He created these scientifically accurate painted collections instead: the tops of the intricate two-part wings, then the undersides, with the elegant little black bodies holding the structure together. There they were, sample after sample, butterfly after butterfly, painted side by side and in columns, art imitating lifelessness, just as if the painter had copied an exhibit from a glass case in some nineteenth-century natural history museum.

If you love butterflies too much to take their lives, why would you paint them as if they were dead? Tiny corpses, captive under glass? Why not paint them in nature, fluttering about in their own haunts and habitats? I keep wondering whether Uncle Walter originally just borrowed somebody else's chloroformed-and-pinned butterfly collection and reproduced it with paint on paper.

In any case, Walter Gifford's butterflies made their way into Alice's family collection, and now have gone on to one of Nat's cousins, to become part of her own aggregate of personal possessions, perhaps to be passed along to a child or a grandchild. With luck, they might eventually wind up with someone like Phoebe, who has been to bug camp, and knows how to pay attention to butterflies, and understands when it is time to let things go.

MIGRATIONS

Where did my eyelashes go?

Didn't I have eyelashes? I mean, more than just a few, sparsely scattered. They've always been up there, haven't they? They used to be attached to my eyelids in some quantity, with enough thickness available to pull on when I got a speck of dust in my eye, in that special way of pulling I was taught as a child—you grabbed the lashes between thumb and forefinger and pulled the eyelid out and over, onto the top of the cheek almost, and then let it go and the speck (usually) was gone.

The other day I had something in my eye and I tried that eyelash-pulling remedy, but it was really hard because the eyelashes themselves were gone. It was as if somebody had come along and pruned them like little carrot seedlings in the vegetable garden, taking every other plant. Pruned eyelashes.

But I *need* them, I thought. I need them to protect me from the specks of dust, and pet hairs, and bits of grit and sand that are kicked up to eye level by wheels or feet or paws moving quickly in my vicinity. I also have the feeling that they come in handy when I'm blinking. I did quite a lot of blinking after undergoing brain surgery a few years ago, though I don't blink quite so often now. Besides, I'm used to having eyelashes, although I suppose I've never done much for them or with them. I'm not an eyelash-batter, and it's been many years since I used mascara and eyeliner, mostly because I never really got the hang of it and always ended up looking less like the wide-eyed beauty featured on the eye makeup ads and more like a startled baby raccoon.

I was actually pretty worried about the loss of my eyelashes. How could I have lost my eyelashes? Eye*glasses*, yes. I lose those all the time, but I keep several pairs, and when I lose them, I usually find them again pretty soon. But eyelashes? How and where was I going to find those?

Well, guess what? I did find them. They were on my chin. A few stray lashes had wandered away from home and gone to visit a neighborhood farther south. I realized that that this is just another in a series of migrations around my body, curious appearances and disappearances, alterations and adjustments that have been happening to various parts of myself as I get older. You never know what's going to turn up where, frankly, even though I've had these parts on me for well over half a century now, and you'd think I could count on them to stay put.

But no, clearly I can't. The southward migration of my eyelashes is a case in point. What am I supposed to do with eyelashes on my chin? I don't think I can persuade them to go back where they belong, nor do I want an eyelash implant. And yet, do I fully accept this change? Do I like having my eyelashes where they are now? No, not by the hairs on my chinny, chin, chin, I do not!

So I tweeze them, my chin-lashes, with the same pair of tweezers I used to pluck my eyebrows when they decided to try growing across the bridge of my nose—the nerve of facial hair! I could probably shave the chin-lashes instead, but I'm afraid it would make me feel too much like a teenage boy trying to grow a beard, and I don't want a beard. Besides, didn't somebody used to tell me that shaving makes the hair grow back more thickly, or more bristly? Something like that. I'm trying hard to think of these few little chin-lashes as something feminine, more peach fuzz than five-o-clock shadow.

"What's that on your chin, Grandma?"

"Oh, it's just a little peach fuzz, dear."

I guess you just have to expect things to change on your body over time. I am reminded of my husband's garden scarecrow he'd made many years ago when he first moved to the farm, a figure he'd constructed with crossed sticks and with straw stuffed into an old shirt and a pair of blue jeans he'd discarded, then padded to look like a facsimile of himself, a tall, strong young man with arms waving away all garden predators. One summer not too long ago, though, he noticed that most of the straw in the scarecrow's upper half had sunk down toward its middle, settling in the belly area. He was just about to repair the figure with new straw, improving its physique, when he happened to look down at his own mid-section. Then he decided that the scarecrow's appearance was just about right after all.

There are advantages, actually, to have things disappear that you didn't really want in the first place. I may have to tweeze my chin-lashes, but there are other places that I no longer have to shave as frequently as I used to, and some places that I don't have to shave at all.

The human body changes constantly, starting right from birth. I know that, though if I think too much about it I get dizzy. I certainly don't look much like the pictures of myself from twenty years ago, and twenty years ago I didn't look much like the pictures from twenty years before that, let alone the old photos from summer camp when I was ten years old, or in family group portraits when I was three or four. Yet the person in each of those pictures was definitely me, and so is the person I see in the mirror today, who doesn't look much like any of the other pictures but is nonetheless the same human being in all of them.

We get used to this partly because we don't have a choice, and partly because that's one of the things we humans are supposed to do best: adapt to change. So I am adapting. It's hard to admit that my feet are a couple of sizes larger than they were when I was twenty, whereas I myself am an inch or two shorter and—oh, how I hate to confess this—about twenty pounds heavier. Funny things are happening in funny places, and one of them is that my eyelashes are moving south. They started up on my eyelids, where they lived for many happy years. Then they travelled down to my chin, where they would now reside except that I keep evicting them. Who knows where they're headed next. Florida? Wherever it is, I certainly wish them well, but in the meantime I think I'll keep on tweezing.

GLADIOLAS

My grandmother had a flower garden. So did my mother and my aunt, and sometimes my sister did, too, though she lived in cities for most of her adult life, and had limited gardening opportunities. As I work in my own garden each summer, with dirt and plants and garden tools all around me, I can't help thinking about other women in my family, and other gardens.

I can still see the sloping border of perennials at my grandmother's house in Maine, a cascade of multicolored blooms in tall waving spires and low blossoming clusters, pink and blue and yellow and red and lavender, running along both sides of the grassy path that led from her house down to a beach of rocks and barnacles. The only flower from that garden whose name stuck with me at the time was "snapdragon," because I never understood how it snapped. If I plucked one flower from its stalk of pale pink or blue or yellow blooms, then put my thumb and my forefinger into an upper and a lower part of that flower and moved my fingers up and down, I could see the resemblance to a tiny, dainty, pastel finger-puppet of a dragon, but it seemed far too well-bred to snap.

My grandmother, Elizabeth Morrow, was like the snapdragon: a small, energetic, warm-hearted woman with very good manners, but, when you looked more closely, had the strong will of a much more imposing creature. I remember her with affection and some clarity, though she died when I was nine years old. Raised modestly in Cleveland, Ohio, and educated at Smith College, she married Dwight Morrow, an Amherst classmate and friend of Calvin Coolidge. Morrow became a banker at J. P. Morgan, and when Coolidge was elected president of the United States, he appointed Morrow to serve as ambassador to Mexico. Though both Dwight and Elizabeth Morrow had once imagined themselves in a quieter world—he would teach history, she would write poetry—I suspect that my grandmother must have enjoyed the diplomatic life: the social connections, the organizational complexities, and the parties. She seemed to me, even at the age I was when I knew her, to love parties. Her gardens, too, were like elaborate, formal parties: well-conceived, well-staffed horticultural galas—my grandmother employed gardeners—with everybody invited except the weeds.

When my cousin Elisabeth inherited the Guest House, a small, beautifully designed New England cape that was built just a short walk from the big house through a wooded area on my grandmother's Maine property, she shared with me the estate's records from 1928 and 1929, when the flower garden for the larger house was being established. I saw orders for 150 "gladioli choice varieties," 40 hosta, 60 annual larkspur, 120 "petunia Rosy Morn," 36 hollyhocks, and more. Mount Desert Nurseries, which supplied the plants for my grandmother's property and other summer places during those years, listed no fewer than 65 varieties of flowers, trees, and shrubs on the invoice. What I remember as a cascade of blossoms was more like a torrent.

I am confused about the gladiolas, though. On the one hand, according to the records, my grandmother chose to have 150 gladiolas planted in her Maine garden. On the other hand, I have always heard that my grandmother and her two sisters, Annie and Edith, disliked gladiolas so much that they made a lifelong pact: when one of the sisters died, the survivor or survivors would see to it that there were no gladiolas at the funeral. Aunt Edith, the youngest and last of the sisters to survive, took this obligation so much to heart that at my grandmother's funeral, Edith went around the church ripping gladiolas from all the floral arrangements.

My aunt Constance, my mother's youngest sister, was a gardener too, though what I remember about her are not her perennials but her love of flowering trees. She was a writer and a scholar, and one of her daughters told me that when Aunt Con pointed out certain trees to her children, she often recited a poem. For the wild cherry tree growing between two northwest evergreens on the farm in Ridgefield, Washington where she lived, she quoted A. E. Housman:

> Loveliest of trees, the cherry now
> Is hung with bloom along the bough.
> (A. E. Housman, "A Shropshire Lad II," stanza 1)

The lilacs near her house evoked Walt Whitman:

> When lilacs last in the dooryard bloom'd,
> And the great star early droop'd in the western sky in the night.
> (Walt Whitman, "When Lilacs Last in the Dooryard Bloom'd," stanza 1)

When the chestnut trees stood in the full glory of their autumnal bronze, she recited Longfellow's "The Village Blacksmith":

> Under a spreading chestnut-tree
> The village smithy stands;
> The smith, a mighty man is he,
> With large and sinewy hands;
> And the muscles of his brawny arms
> Are strong as iron bands.
> (Henry Wadsworth Longfellow, "The Village Blacksmith," stanza 1)

As far as I know, Aunt Con did not plant gladiolas. Neither did my mother, in the modest annual and perennial beds she tended near our home in southern Connecticut. She planted bulbs in the fall, and there were always flowering shrubs blooming near our house in spring. She wore gardening gloves when she worked outdoors and carried a pair of clippers on walks along the roads of our suburban neighborhood near Long Island Sound, when she would frequently clip the occasional roadside branch and carry it along with her. Our neighborhood roadsides were unkempt and brambly in those days, with marsh and thicket alternating, and big old houses just visible at the ends of long winding driveways off the main road.

It didn't occur to me that as she walked and clipped my mother was, in effect, pruning her neighbors' property without permission. I just thought of her as a kind of self-appointed caretaker for the local landscape, trimming branches and picking up sticks in her path. The sticks were obstacles she laid to one side so that the next walker would not stumble. The branches, though, were beautiful, so she took those home. She would put a purloined branch in a tall, thin-necked vase or in a fat-bellied dark green Chianti bottle, emptied of wine and filled with water. She might set one of these on her writing desk for inspiration, or on a windowsill in order to display the graceful shape of the reaching twigs against the sky. She told me the names of the trees and shrubs the branches had come from: "forsythia," or "euonymus," always words that were hard to pronounce and easy to forget, but she didn't mind how many times I asked.

Then there were my mother's rose bushes, planted by a low, curved stone wall on a hill away from the house. I think some of these bushes came from my grandmother's rose garden after her death. I don't remember a profusion of blooms, but instead one breathtaking pink rose at a time, its soft petals unfolding, its scent filling the air as my mother came through the door holding a rose in one garden-gloved hand and her clippers in the other.

Sometimes she cut her roses only a few inches below the bloom, with one or two leaves and several thorns remaining on the stem. The thorns were surprisingly sharp. I can still almost feel the one that pierced the ball of my unwary thumb one day, can still see the drop of blood slowly emerging, can still remember my shocked and trembling surprise. How had such pain come from my mother's roses?

There were pansies, lots of them, sad little dog-faced flowers with velvety petals. They grew along the walk and at the base of a Japanese maple tree with multiply-pointed red leaves. The pansies were mostly light blue or yellow, but sometimes, and best, they were a midnight purple, almost black, with a tiny bit of yellow at the center. They had short, yielding stems so I could pick them with my fingers easily. Someone had told me that the more you picked pansies, the more they would bloom, so I brought fistfuls of them into the house for my mother to arrange in water glasses or, if I'd picked too close to the flower head, to float in a bowl on a table. They didn't float too well and were quickly swamped, like tiny waterlogged lilies sinking into a very small pond.

Daffodils bloomed on the lawn in spring, and narcissus, too, which I preferred. Even though the two were similar and grew in the same places, the narcissus was more delicate and had a more appealing fragrance. In among the trees and in shady places there was myrtle, which my mother also called "vinca" or "periwinkle," a low ground-cover that carpeted the whole area with its small dark green leaves and even smaller blue flowers. Growing near them were lilies of the valley, with broad leaves and thin, bending stalks from which hung perhaps a dozen little white bells.

My paternal grandmother, in Detroit, had lilies of the valley in her garden, too. I hardly knew my grandmother Lindbergh, my father's mother. When we visited her I was a very young child, and she was in bed, suffering from Parkinson's disease. She died in 1954, when I was nine years old. My other grandmother, Grandmother Morrow or "Grandma Bee," died following a stroke only a few months later, but I feel as if I knew her very well. My mother's mother was a very active grandmother. She loved to have her grandchildren with her, as many of them as possible, in Maine in the summer, in Mexico during the years when she had a house there, and in Englewood whenever they could come throughout the year. Her house in New Jersey was only an hour or so from ours in Connecticut, and our family piled in a station wagon for Thanksgiving dinner and on many Sundays, enjoying her large house, Next Day Hill, with its sloping lawns and elegant tall trees outdoors, its brushy woodland with a little running brook just the right size to explore, and indoors its long hallways and curved staircase, the fingerbowls and butterballs and real silver on the long, well-polished dining room table. There was a cook called Elsie who lived, I thought, somewhere behind the swinging door to the kitchen; there were maids in black uniforms with white aprons busying themselves all over the house, and there was a butler named James who liked children. There was a gardener there, too, and a garden where the rosebushes grew, and well-tended box-bushes all around the building, with a scent I will never forget. Our small Morrow grandmother twinkled at us all, and the whole household seemed ordered and commanded around our visits. She liked to read to us in the evenings, all gathered around the soft blue armchair in her study.

My Lindbergh grandmother was completely different. She did not move around and she did not twinkle, but instead lay pale and almost motionless in her bed in her dark house in the city of Detroit. Whenever she spoke, it was hard to understand what she said. She had a very sweet smile, though, especially when she looked at my father.

When my brother Scott and I went outside from this house into the sunshine once, I remember it being so bright by contrast that I wanted to go right back indoors again, but at the same time, I desperately did not. Indoors was too dark and mysterious for me, in every way. At that time I didn't know anything about my father's family at all.

My father told me more than once that his father, my grandfather, was said to be the best-looking man in Minnesota. Once in a while he passed on sayings of my grandfather Lindbergh's that made him chuckle, but that I didn't understand. For instance: "One boy is a boy, two boys are half a boy, and three boys are no boy at all." I finally figured out that this meant boys got into more trouble when they were in groups, but I already knew that. I had three brothers.

I learned more from my father's writing than from him about his parents. In a little book, really a long letter to a friend, about his childhood in Minnesota, my father revealed that his father taught him to swim in Pike Creek, near their home, and in the Mississippi River, which was of a relatively modest size near Little Falls. Doing the breaststroke, my father wrote, his father had carried him on his back. I remembered that my father had done exactly the same thing with me when I was learning to swim, in Scott's Cove of Long Island Sound. He did the breaststroke out into the cove, and I held onto his shoulders.

I discovered from the same little book that my father's mother loved flowers, planting lilac and honeysuckle bushes along the road in front of the house in Little Falls. He mentions violets and nasturtiums, as well as beds filled largely with irises, which, he guesses, were probably her favorite flower. Irises are probably my favorite flower, too, and I love our lilac bushes, some of them planted long before my husband and I came to our farm. When I first read my father's brief Minnesota memoir, one of the most personal pieces of writing of his lifetime, I wished that I had really known my grandmother Evangeline, had not just seen her in passing, as it were, when her life was almost over. I wished especially that I had been able to spend time with her while she was gardening.

Where I live now I have lilies of the valley growing under the big maple tree in what I call my "shade garden," near the pond, and they seem to love this one shady place. They have multiplied to make a small colony for themselves, keeping company with several hardy clumps of violets and a staunch contingent of the attractive low-growing ground cover called *Pulmonaria*, with the unfortunate common name "lungwort." There are a few newly transplanted hosta plants in that same area, doing very well so far, and one robust astilbe with glossy green leaves and waving, feathery red plumes.

And, with apologies to my maternal ancestors but with thanks to my husband who planted them, I have gladiolas. I love gladiolas. What glorious, riotous blooms they are, planted on a grassy hillside behind the pond and offering to the world their wild show of red, yellow, orange, pink, magenta, and blue. I see them as fiery, not funereal, and if the display is a little gaudy, well, as my husband said, "We can use a little 'gaudy' in this climate." It seems outrageous that any flowers so exotically colorful could bloom here in northern Vermont. I am grateful to the gladiolas because they do.

Gardening is largely a matter of gratitude for me anyway. I am grateful to the flowers that grow in my garden, persistent and forgiving. No matter what I do to them or forget to do for them, the perennials appear in the same places every spring. By now I should know this is going to happen, but I never quite believe it.

I've lived on this farm for more than thirty years now, and the garden has yet to fail me. Even when I myself have sunk all the way down to the bottom of the middle of January, when the whole cold world outside seems white and vast and without form or promise—even then the flowers have plans. They are biding their time under the bird feeder and behind the fence and around the big maple tree, waiting for spring to come, because it will.

And it does. After the snow melts and the mud season has come and gone, the earth warms and the flowers come up through the ground again, uninterested in my midwinter pessimism or in my giddy May-time joy at the miracle of their return. They have work to do: stems to grow, buds to nurture, blooms to put forth into the air, just as the flowers did when my mother was clipping her neighbor's forsythia and my aunt was reciting poetry to trees and my grandmother was inviting gladiolas to the festivity of her perennial borders, but not to her funeral.

I am glad that my flowers bloom and prosper, that they repeat themselves, reminding me of all that is recurrent in life: hollyhocks by my door and lilies of the valley under the maple tree recalling the ones in my grandmothers' gardens; my daughter's forehead that reminds me so much of my mother's; lilacs blooming by my window like the ones near my Aunt Con's house; my niece's blue-eyed, impish smile that makes me think of her mother, my sister Anne; an occasional look or gesture in my son Ben that is so like my brother Scott it stops me in mid-thought.

One August day, our family gathered at our home in memory of my husband's oldest son, my stepson Eli, who had died suddenly that spring at the age of thirty-six at his home in Montana. He had spent his childhood summers and vacations here and returned often during his adult years, bringing along his wife and his young family. Many relatives and friends came together this day to remember him. We stood in a circle on the grass at noon, while some people spoke about him and others stood silent, thinking perhaps of his long battle with cystic fibrosis that finally took his life. I saw Eli's two children, his six-year-old twin son and daughter, standing quietly with their mother. They were squinting into the midday sun on the same grassy lawn between the house and the pond where their father had run and shrieked and chased and been chased by other children over the years. I could imagine him jumping into the hammock that hung between the two maples, and wading with a net, thigh-high in muddy water, looking for frogs in the pond. I could see him striking off alone, up the dirt road and into the high fields to explore the woods beyond.

I was kept present on that heartbreaking and beautiful day by looking at what remained of my summer garden: deep pink phlox near the house; blowsy yellow heads of golden glow by the fence; a tall blue spire or two of late delphinium at the back of the border. Then I saw something that caught my understanding and held it suspended in that moment of pain and confusion and shock and, perhaps, some shared ache toward reverence, distributed from generation to generation through our hands in the earth of our gardens, wherever they may be. Across the pond, above a green slope, the sun picked out one red gladiola blossom and transformed it, giving the flower for just a few instants a different color entirely, an almost transparent blood-crimson, not representative of anything I could remember or put a name to. But it offered me exactly what I wanted to look at in that place and at that time, like an ancient stained-glass window fragment in bright light.

MUD SEASON
AND BEYOND

After a long winter, at the end of March or in early April, I forget that spring is inevitable; it really will come. I'm impatient, and I wish I could do something to make it come *now*. I remember having the same feeling as a child growing up in Connecticut, on Long Island Sound, where spring came a month earlier than it does here in northern Vermont. Still, for me it never came soon enough. One year I went around outside my home with warm water in a pitcher, possibly the same water pitcher I now have in my kitchen, with the words "Allegheny Metal Ware" engraved on its base. (I don't know what metal it is made of—not silver, not pewter—maybe steel? There was a steeliness to the whole 1950s, as I remember it: railroad tracks, the braces on my teeth, the color of my father's hair, the glint in his eye when he had something serious to say to me or to anyone else in the family.) I walked around the house with a possibly steel pitcher full of warm water, and I poured the water on stubbornly wintry things: icy spears of grass along the front path, frozen mud-puddles in the driveway. I wanted to do my bit to break the grip of winter on New England. I wanted to thaw the whole world.

Here in early April, it is almost spring, or, at least, it should be. What it really is, as any Vermont native will tell you, is Mud Season. After a harsh February, with sub-zero temperatures lasting for days and sometimes weeks at a time, and a tantalizing March with alternating snowfall and snowmelt, suddenly we have daytime temperatures in the fifties, heavy slabs of snow sliding off the roof in a series of thunderous thumps, almost impassably muddy roads, and a porous white landscape of softened snow covering our lawn, dotted plentifully by lumps of dog poop.

That's what you get when you have two dogs, neither of them particularly modest about their bodily functions. This may be our fault. We lavished praise on these pets as puppies every time they made their deposits outdoors rather than on the living room carpet. Now like children who have not yet outgrown the need for applause at their every accomplishment, they squat with pride much too close to the house and gaze at us with shining eyes as they do their business. Look, Mom!

Our lawn in early April isn't a pretty sight. This is not yet the time of burgeoning and blooming, which arrives a month later, in mid-May. This is the time of disintegration and dissolution. In a few weeks, the poop will be indistinguishable, thank goodness, from last autumn's unraked maple leaves, which have now blackened and lost all form and turned into a dark and flattened overall wetness. Everything is absorbed into the soil in the general nihilism of the season before anything can start again.

And it does start again. Nothing, not even the mess on the lawn, can hold back the new season, not even the discouraging late frosts of April and early May. During these days, impatient as ever, I know that the only thing I can do is to wait. However long it may take, however ugly our yard may look until the process is complete, I wait until everything is thoroughly absorbed into the leaf mulch of the lawn, and the lawn itself is dry enough so that I can begin. Then, I rake. I gather up armfuls of leaves and twigs and sticks, hold them between the fan-spread tines of the rake and my own splayed fingers, and walk across the driveway to the leaves-and-sticks pile under the lilac bush, where I let them all fall. Then I go back over to the lawn and do it again.

I can do this for hours, raking up and carrying away last year's leaves and vines and long dead blooms, feeling the sun and the wind, gently combing the soil that holds the promise of this year's new growth. I don't know whether my raking really helps the season or the yard at all, any more than my determined warm-water pouring helped to banish winter long ago. I only know that the raking helps me, encouraging a change from my winter moods and indoor habits. I stretch out my body along with my rake, uncover the waiting possibilities of flowers and plants that won't bloom for a month or two yet, (echinacea, globe thistle, delphinium, cushion spurge), hear the Baltimore oriole singing in the maple tree overhead and watch a pair of mallard ducks who have returned to the pond again this year, as in so many years past. I stretch and rake and recognize and name things to myself, and I'm happy.

My mother used to talk about the need for human beings to affirm what she called "the ongoingness of life," to find a way to move along with change and become part of it, season after season, year after year, even during times of great trouble: the need to celebrate the arrival of a new baby, for example, the very month that a beloved family member has just died. I understood this when I first glimpsed my younger daughter after her birth in early January, six months after my father's death. I saw that she had a dimple in her chin, like my father's. Tiny, intensely blue-eyed, stunned as I was by the enormity of her own birth, her view of the world not yet focused with recognition of anything I knew, still she had his dimple.

Family recognitions and confusions are not uncommon at such moments. I think of the illness and death of my sister, Anne, whom we called "Ansy" in the family, from cancer more than twenty years ago. She was very brave, very funny, and very present for as long as she could be, until at the end morphine and the disease itself took her into another place of fantasy and dreams and, I think, nightmares too—it was hard to tell during those last days. Our mother, also named Anne, was in fragile health at the time and often confused, though as far as I could tell, she was not in pain. Because my mother rarely spoke, I was under the impression for a while that she did not understand how perilous her older daughter's medical state was.

Then, one day, she said to me unexpectedly out of her habitual silence, "It is the wrong name on the door." I took this to mean that she understood completely, and wanted to express her passionate sense that the wrong Anne was dying. My sister was then 53 years old, her children not yet grown to adulthood; my mother was 87. That winter, my thoughts raced and sputtered back and forth between the two of them like an overcharged current in a damaged electrical system.

My sister died, my mother lived for another seven years, my children grew up with Ansy's son and daughter, who remained very close to our family. Ansy's son got his driver's license, her daughter continued at college, Ansy's husband married again after several sad years as a widower. Later, my daughters and Ansy's daughter married, and now there are grandchildren, mine and Ansy's too. I celebrate their births for both of us.

The first year after Ansy's death, I didn't even know how to celebrate my own birth, because my birthday is the same day as hers. I was born five years later but on the same day, and we had always celebrated together. I didn't know how to have a birthday without her. My family helped me to find a way, and now we keep the double birthday and call it "Ansy Reeve Day" on the calendar.

After my sister died, I literally moved in her footsteps for a while, because I was wearing her socks. Not long after Ansy's death that cold winter, her daughter gave me a colorful woolen pair Ansy had knitted herself. I wore them constantly, except when I washed them, and they kept my feet warm until eventually I wore a hole in one of them. I became despondent, and wrote in my journal, "I hate it that I can wear a hole in her sock, and she's not here to show me how to fix it!" I had no idea how to darn a sock myself. Then I figured it out, more or less. I worked over the hole by weaving back and forth with a darning needle and some bright-colored yarn until I had made the necessary, if lumpy, repairs. Then I put my sister's socks back on my feet and went on walking.

Knitting and darning in winter are not as effective or satisfying physically as reaching and raking are in the spring, but they, too, constitute movement. That helps. I know a woman who skied down a mountain over and over again during the winter of her divorce, weeping on the chairlift that took her to the summit, immersing herself in the rhythms and momentum of skiing down to the bottom, then going up and doing it all over again. I know another woman who hiked most of the Presidential mountain range when her own marriage broke up in the late summer and fall of another year. My husband ran for miles every day over dirt roads one spring until he exhausted himself, at the time when his first marriage had dissolved and his young son had been diagnosed with a terminal disease.

Now, in midsummer, my husband has been working in his vegetable garden every day, preparing the ground to grow the food he will offer the two of us, and any visiting friends or family members, all summer long. His fragile young plants (tomatoes, peppers, eggplant) are still indoors in their pots by the window. These vegetables were grown from the seeds he planted indoors in early March. Nat and many other citizens of this state start the seedlings on the first Tuesday of that month, which is also Town Meeting Day all over Vermont. Almost three months later, on or about Memorial Day in May, the other seeds go in the garden by hand, carefully, row by row. My husband is more comfortable wearing shorts, heavy-duty khaki or army green ones, at this time of year, and he works on his hands and knees. This is the beginning of the season when his knees are covered with dirt for most of the day, something I welcome as a sign of his deep content.

The seeds for the garden, many packets of them, most often come in the mail from companies like Johnny's or Fedco in Maine, but he also picks up some from the racks at the local hardware store. Before planting begins, the seed packets are laid out before him like a deck of cards on one end of the kitchen table and I can read the labels: Christmas Lima Pole Beans; Hybrid Okra Jambalaya; Laurentian Rutabaga; Bibb Lettuce; Early Summer Yellow Crookneck Squash; Helena Muskmelon; Arcadia Broccoli; Silver Queen Corn. He is very happy, and I know it's not just because of the seeds themselves and the vegetables they represent, but because of the work ahead.

Planting, cultivating, weeding, harvesting, all the labor he will be required to perform outdoors every day pleases him, however tiring it may be, after a long winter spent mainly indoors. There is the vegetable garden, and working in the woods, then the haying, a winter's worth of hay to bring in for our sheep, who don't eat much by the standards of "real" (dairy) farmers, but who need enough feed to keep us and a couple of teenage helpers busy on sunny summer afternoons. We may be busy all summer, in fact, due to the vagaries of both weather and our ancient haying equipment. Mower, tedder, baler, and tractor are all vulnerable to breakdowns, and each machine has its own special quirks. Nat will often make the repairs himself, or if not he'll find someone else who can, so we go on making hay while the sun shines, if it does. Some summers are sunnier than others, but haying goes on anyway, intermittently, well into August. We struggle through it, suffer over it, Nat curses the equipment and the rain, and aches a lot at night. I maintain that he loves it all, anyway, that for him this is the same body-love that I experience in a much quieter way in my raking, an exuberance of participation in sheer being.

He is there, and I am here, after the dog poop has dissolved and the seeds are about to be planted. On the lawn, the dead leaves are ready for me to rake away from the new grass growing, and the tantalizing, invisible, but nonetheless present oriole is singing overhead.

SEEING THE
AIRPLANES

My mother never flew in the *Spirit of St. Louis*. This always seemed odd to me, although I knew that my father's most famous aircraft was built to hold just one person, the pilot, and that there wasn't much room to spare inside that cockpit. The idea was to carry enough fuel for the 1927 flight from New York to Paris—with a little to spare—and to save weight in every other way. Some people called the *Spirit* "a flying gas tank," because that's pretty much what it was. It certainly was not designed to carry passengers.

Still, in the flight log my father kept for the *Spirit*, a number of people are listed as having flown with him in that plane—one at a time, and usually for no longer than ten or fifteen minutes, twenty at longest. Having looked into the very compact cockpit, where my father's six feet, two inches must have felt confined already, I've always wondered where he put these people. On his lap? And how hard was it to fly the plane with somebody else in there with him?

According to aviation legend, the *Spirit of St. Louis* was not an easy plane to fly, with or without passengers. I once heard a story about the creation of the *Spirit of St. Louis* flying replica in the 1950s, for the film in which Jimmy Stewart played my father. Apparently the people who built the replica had followed the original specifications very carefully, and believed that they had successfully copied the airplane. However, when their plane was finished and it was time for the first test flights, something seemed terribly wrong.

The replica was unstable in the air, the test pilot reported. It shook and shuddered constantly. If the pilot allowed his attention to stray for even an instant, the Spirit would stray off course. What had they missed?

While those responsible for construction were still pondering this, my father himself visited the set. He wanted to see the flying replica of the *Spirit*; in fact, he hoped to fly it. After a certain amount of discussion and concern and maybe even a little panic, the decision was made to let him fly the replica just as it was. After all, he knew a thing or two about the original *Spirit*—maybe he could figure out how to correct the mistakes that had been made in building this one.

My father took off in the *Spirit* replica while a group of anxious people waited on the ground below. He was gone for five minutes, then he was gone for ten minutes. The people on the ground expected at any moment to see him bring the plane down, upset and disappointed. But he was gone for a long time before he finally brought the little plane in to land.

Everyone waited anxiously to hear his thoughts, and when he emerged from the cockpit, he exclaimed, "I had forgotten what a *wonderful* little plane that was!"

And then, "And you got it—you got it perfectly, in every detail!"

Whatever its charms or flaws, the original *Spirit of St. Louis* carried quite a few people as passengers during the year it was in the air, from April 1927 to April 1928, at which point the aircraft was donated to the Smithsonian Institution for permanent exhibit. Many of those passengers flew before the New York to Paris flight, during test flights of the plane in late April and early May of 1927. Some of them were on board for final checking and safety purposes; others, presumably, for Ryan Airlines's own design and business records. (The San Diego-based aircraft company Ryan Airlines, with my father's help, designed and built the aircraft in just under sixty days.)

After the flight to Paris, when the plane had become as famous as its pilot, some notable individuals are listed in the flight log as passengers, including Henry Ford, on August 11, 1927, flying from Ford Airport in Detroit, Michigan. This was Henry Ford's first flight in an airplane.

For August 12, 1927, from the same airport, my father records, "One flight, carrying Mother." That would be his mother, not mine. He carried a few more passengers during that fall, including Earl C. Thompson, a St. Louis backer of the flight; Virginia Governor Harry F. Byrd; and my father's lifelong friend, the philanthropist and aviation supporter Harry F. Guggenheim. Then in December, my father flew the airplane from the United States to Mexico for a brief but significant visit.

He began his trip to Mexico in Washington, DC, and as he flew along he followed his customary practice of finding his way in the United States using road maps and local landmarks, such as railroad stations that bore the names of the towns he was passing over. In those days he could simply follow railroad tracks from town to town to figure out where he was.

When he crossed the border into Mexico, therefore, in order to confirm his route, it seemed reasonable to fly low over a railroad station. When he looked for the name of the town, he saw this word: "Caballeros."

He checked the Mexican road map for the location. Strangely, he could not find any town called "Caballeros" there at all. He then flew to the next town, found the railroad station, and discovered another sign.

It too read, "Caballeros."

My father confessed that he flew over three Mexican towns before he realized that "Caballeros" meant "men's room."

Despite this setback, he made his way to Mexico City, where he was greeted by enthusiastic crowds and welcomed by his host, Ambassador Dwight Morrow, and by the Morrow family, including Elizabeth Morrow, their son Dwight Morrow, Jr., and their three daughters: Elisabeth, Constance, and Anne—my mother.

At this point, my father and his plane were famous worldwide, and crowds often overran the airfields wherever the *Spirit* landed. In Mexico, it was considered essential for public safety, as well as the preservation of the airplane itself, to keep the aircraft secured in a hangar, out of sight and inaccessible, even to my mother and her family.

Although she never was one of its passengers, the *Spirit of St. Louis* literally brought my parents together. She had come home from college for Christmas, and my father, with his mother, had been invited to spend the holiday with the Morrow family at the beginning of my father's goodwill tour through Latin America to promote aviation. My mother met him at a formal reception, seeing, as she later wrote in a diary, "a tall, slim boy in evening dress—so much slimmer, so much taller, so much more poised than I expected." He spent several days with the family, and took my mother and her sisters flying in a big silver five-passenger Ford plane that had brought his own mother to Mexico.

He took my mother flying again in October of 1928 in a De Havilland Moth, flying out of a horse pasture at Harry Guggenheim's home in Long Island. Their engagement was announced in February of 1929, and a few months later, my parents were married. The ceremony took place in the Morrow home, Next Day Hill, in Englewood, New Jersey, on May 27, 1929, with only family members and close friends present.

My father taught my mother to fly, and by her own account she loved it. She loved glider flying above all, which she learned to do in San Diego with my father in 1930. She wrote to her mother of the experience: "It was so delicious, so still . . . I heard a bird singing." My mother became the first licensed woman glider pilot in the United States. She also became a skilled airplane pilot, navigator, and radio operator, critical skills in the survey flights my parents undertook for what was to become Pan American Airways. For one of these flights, they traveled over the North Pole to Asia in 1931, in a modified Lockheed Sirius seaplane they named *Tingmissartoq*, for an Inuit word called out to them by children, meaning "one who flies like a big bird." She wrote about this adventure in her book *North to the Orient*, which received the National Book Award for Nonfiction in 1936, the first year the award was offered.

In his foreword to another of her books about their flights together, *Listen! The Wind*, my father wrote, "There were no facilities for aircraft at most of the places where we landed." Of course there weren't. My parents were flying together to discover the places where those facilities should be located. They were pioneers of air travel before either one of them had reached the age of thirty, and the people in the places where they landed were often astonished to see them, never before having received visitors by air.

My mother wrote that in places like Aklavik and Point Barrow, Alaska, people could not grow vegetables at all. Most of their provisions came in by boat once a year around the tip of Alaska from Nome. For a brief period in the summer, the icy waters were clear enough for a boat to reach Point Barrow, but even then, the ice pack might make it impossible. As they were leaving Point Barrow, my father found an orange in the pocket of his flying suit, and offered it to one of the women there, a doctor's wife. According to my mother, the woman "held it in her palms for a moment as though warming her hands by its glow."

This was one of the many miracles that aviation offered to remote corners of the world: the promise of fresh food, the blessing of communication, the end of a kind of isolation that had been the condition of life in such places for centuries. My parents were mapping out the shortest, most efficient air routes in the world, which had never been done before. What an adventure!

It must have been reassuring to know that the *Tingmissartoq*, built by the Lockheed Company to my father's exact specifications and completed in 1930, was so well designed and supplied for the journeys ahead. My mother includes eight pages in the appendix of *North to the Orient* devoted to equipment and provisions, from revolvers and ammunition to mosquito nets, canned tomatoes, bilge pumps, and long underwear (two pairs).

Fully prepared and provisioned, they began their journeys: first over the North Pole, and a few years later—following the tragic death of their first child, Charles, and the birth of their second one, my brother Jon—exploring Greenland and Iceland, touring northern Europe and Russia, then heading south for the Azores and Africa, then home across the South Atlantic.

My mother was the first woman pilot to cross both the North and South Atlantic in an open-cockpit airplane. As much as she loved these flights, and as eloquently as she wrote about them, my mother did not fly with her husband in the *Tingmissartoq* for very many years. At the end of 1933, with their aerial surveys complete, my parents donated the Lockheed Sirius and all its equipment ("down to [their] can of insect repellant,"[8] as biographer A. Scott Berg notes) to the American Museum of Natural History in New York, where it was displayed for several years in the Hall of Ocean Life. Then the plane went to the Air Force Museum in Ohio, and finally found its present home at the Smithsonian's National Air and Space Museum in Washington, not far from the *Spirit of St. Louis.*

The provisions listed in *North to the Orient* remind me not of my mother, since when I knew her she mostly wrote letters and books, not lists (except for groceries or recipes), but of my father and his endless list-making during the intermittent periods when he was home during my childhood. He used a knife-sharpened number two pencil with the lead protruding perhaps an eighth of an inch, and a pad of lightweight light blue airmail paper, and he listed by hand everything he intended to do, everyone he intended to write, every chore his children should be directed to perform, and every fault or flaw that each one of his offspring should be reminded to correct. I remember that each child's list was headed with that child's name, underlined, and that some lists were dauntingly longer than others.

How frustrating child-rearing must have been for my father, as compared to flying an airplane. Surely making and checking the lists of supplies for the survey flights must have been infinitely more satisfactory, along with all of his pre-flight checklists as a pilot in the early days. Marriage, too, must have been difficult, so unlike any previous experience in his life. My father virtually grew up an only child. He had two much older half-sisters from his father's first marriage, but he rarely saw them. His mother and father separated when he was very young, and he lived most of the time with his mother and sometimes her brother, whom we knew in his later years as a blue-eyed, white-haired, quiet man we called "Uncle," though his name was also Charles.

Daily life with a wife and five children could not have been easy for my father, despite any amount of list-making, though we all tried hard to obey our father and to follow his instructions, and my mother tried to make his life comfortable when he was home. I know from conversations with her during the years after his death that my mother, too, thought it was very hard for my father to be married at all. In one of our conversations late in her life, my mother made the suggestion to me that my father would have been happier "as some kind of warrior monk," roaming the world in pursuit of great adventures.

I agreed with her then, but thinking about him now, I realize that the role of warrior fit him, and the notion of adventures all over the world, but he certainly wasn't a monk. He had many relationships with women, I have learned since his death, but I have also learned that he did not spend a great deal of his time with any of them. He established homes for these women, including my mother, and took financial responsibility for all of his children, visited them for longer or shorter periods, and then he went away again. I suspect that this is the only way he could have had a sustained relationship with a wife and family, or several woman and their families, or anyone at all: like a migratory bird, flying in and flying out regularly, but never able to commit to a single home.

It was both exciting and exhausting to have my father at home, when he was home. The air seemed electric as he moved around the house, filling every room with his six-foot-two-inch presence and his ideas, talking constantly and energetically about whatever thoughts consumed him at the time: the lives of his Swedish forebears during the time before, during, and after they settled in Minnesota; the plight of the endangered blue whale or the Tamaraw (a forty-inch-tall wild buffalo in the Philippines); the vanishing elephants of Africa; the environmental and economic drawbacks to the development of the supersonic transport aircraft, or SST, an aircraft to which he was fundamentally opposed, though it delighted wealthy passengers for a number of years as the *Concorde*, flying from New York to Paris many decades after my father did, much more luxuriously and a great deal faster than the *Spirit* had flown in 1927.

I like to think that my parents' airplanes will always be at the Air and Space Museum when I visit. After eight decades at the Smithsonian, I hope they're not going anywhere else. Don Lopez, former deputy director of the Air and Space Museum, once told me that the *Spirit* was so well maintained and serviced by the institution that it could fly off into the clouds again if it had to. I immediately imagined the Lockheed Sirius following right behind it. They belong together, though they did not ever share the air. The *Spirit of St. Louis* was given to the Smithsonian in April of 1928, while the Lockheed was designed and constructed in Burbank, California, in 1929. The *Spirit's* flying days were over before the *Tingmissartoq* ever left the ground.

During the early part of my own life, these airplanes—in their day examples of state-of-the-art aviation technology—were to me "historic," entirely outside of my own experience in the mid-1950s, and therefore ancient to the point of being primitive, even though I was born only eighteen years after the *Spirit* flew to Paris, and only fourteen years after the Lockheed surveyed the "North Atlantic route" for the fledgling aviation industry. Still, by the time I saw them in the museum, the airplanes seemed to belong centuries back in time. They were like pterodactyls, flying dinosaurs, compared to the passenger jets of my own era.

When I looked at my parents' pioneering aircraft at the Smithsonian, moreover, there was another distortion in perspective. I could not quite accept these airplanes as *real*, even though they were right in front of me, even though they had also appeared in the photographs in my parents' books, with my parents in them. The airplanes were as much a part of our personal family history as the house we lived in when I was growing up, or my grandmother's house in Englewood, New Jersey, where we went for Sunday dinner, down the Merritt Parkway and over the George Washington Bridge. The difference was that the airplanes were not part of *my* own personal history with my family.

I was a young adult before I even read any of my parents' books. My father's book *The Spirit of St. Louis* was published by Scribner in 1954, when I was nine years old, and my mother's *Gift from the Sea* was published by Pantheon Books in 1955, when I was ten. When I read these books for the first time about ten years later, it was as if I could hear my parents talking. When I read the books again, now that both parents have been dead for many years and I am older than they were when they wrote them, their voices are just as clear, and in these voices on the page I find a profound sense of familiarity and comfort. Yes. Here they are, my father and my mother. Here.

Interestingly, I also find my parents now, as I did not find them as a child, when I visit the airplanes at the Smithsonian National Air and Space Museum. The airplanes have come alive for me, along with the flying equipment, the supplies, the artifacts, and the clothing. When my parents were living, these were all dead things, like the tools and implements found at a prehistoric burial site. Now that my parents are dead, though, their possessions in the museums seem to shimmer with recent habitation, as if they had just been used a minute ago, as if I could take them out of the glass case and hold them and immediately detect the mildly floral scent of my mother's hand cream (was it Jergens Lotion?) or the mixture of smells I associated with my father: a tinge of pencil shavings, a hint of motor oil or kerosene, wet and trampled oak leaves, and always a clean white cotton handkerchief.

On one of my most recent visits to the museum, Dorothy Cochrane, curator in the Aeronautics department, showed me some of my mother's clothing from the days when she was flying with my father—not the flying clothes but those she wore on the ground. I don't remember my mother ever wearing those flapper dresses and hats, or sporting the bobbed hair I've seen in photos of her from the 1930s in the books of her diaries and letters that have been published over the years. I never saw my parents' flying suits at all, at least, not in person. Those were already in museums by the time I was born, part of public history but not part of real life, not my life.

I saw a photo of a pair of my mother's boots, worn on the 1933 survey flight around the North Atlantic, and listed tersely in her account of that adventure as "1 pr. Kamiks, sealskin and dogskin lined (Eskimo boots)." In *North to the Orient*, my mother describes receiving and wearing these same boots, a gift from the Eskimo people of Point Barrow when the *Tingmissartoq* landed there: "Over two pairs of heavy double-weight socks I pulled on the boots they had given me. Made of sealskin, sewed and chewed into shape by the Eskimo women, they were the warmest, driest, lightest shoes I have ever worn."[9]

I realized at once that the boots, which to my eye looked big for my mother's size five feet, must have been exactly right with those heavy-weight socks inside them. Were they wool socks? They must have been, in that era. We used to wear two pairs of socks when we went skiing with my parents. My father directed that we should have one pair of lightweight socks and one pair of heavier ones, not two layers of thick wool. He insisted that a light layer and a heavy layer would give our toes sufficient warmth and more room for movement and blood circulation. Maybe he learned this lesson on the flight over the North Pole, or possibly during those winters in Minnesota.

Dorothy Cochrane showed me images of other items of family clothing from the same period. There were hats and scarves and dresses of my mother's, some of my father's gloves and boots, even one of my Lindbergh grandmother's dresses. It was a dark blue silk dress, quite short, elegant, and timeless. It gave me the feeling that she had a real sense of style, something I had never known or guessed. Though a little rumpled in the way clothes are that have not been worn for a long time, all it needed was the touch of a warm iron and somebody could wear it to a party.

In a context like this I often feel, again, a kind of dizzying double view of my family. This dress is an artifact from another era; it is part of a story that fascinated the world, a carefully preserved and itemized historical property. But at the same time, this is my grandmother's dress. It was real—she wore it. What on earth is it doing in the National Air and Space Museum? Shouldn't it be in a chest in a family attic, with other attic things? Old skis, unused mahogany bureaus, ancient oil paintings, and dressmaker's dummies?

When I looked at the photograph of the dress, I had the same feeling I have experienced recently when looking at the equipment and the clothing from the airplanes, that this was part of somebody's wardrobe, somebody's life, and much closer to me than I have ever appreciated before.

I used to keep the museums at arm's length, wanting to maintain the distance between the public story and my private recollections. Now, at this time in my life, I go looking for the very things I used to try to stay away from: the airplanes, the artifacts, the old stories, any and all bits and pieces of the past. That careful, strict separation between my family life at home and my parents' life in the historical world seems less clear, and less necessary. I've found that there is even a certain sweetness in discovering traces of what I knew in an unexplored location: a museum, a university, a town I have not visited before, just as there is sweetness in finding a touch of my mother or my sister in my daughters—that high forehead, that quizzical twist of the mouth—or a look of my father in my son.

I think I have found in visiting the airplanes a kind of understanding of my parents' marriage that I didn't comprehend when I was growing up. I knew that my father was away from home more than other fathers seemed to be, and I was aware that it could be difficult for the whole family, including my mother, when he was home, walking and talking with so much energy and taking control of the house which she managed perfectly well in her gentle manner when he was away.

I don't think that the years of my childhood were, for my parents, at all like the years when they flew over the world together in the *Tingmissartoq*. I loved the home my family shared with my mother and father, and the life we had growing up in Connecticut, even with my father coming and going so often, even though the times when he was home were full of unexpected excitements and disturbances. All the same, thinking about it now, I understand why my brother Land once said thoughtfully, long after both of our parents had died: "They never should have stopped flying."

STILL WRITING

One of the things people talk about when they meet is what they do for a living. "What kind of law do you practice?" "What are you teaching this semester?" And you're off and running.

If you are a writer, though, conversation can be a little trickier. One of the questions I am often asked is, "What are you working on these days?" It's a friendly query, easiest to answer when I'm actually working on something. Then I can say, as I have done in the past, "I'm finishing up a project with my family, collecting my mother's unpublished diaries and letters" or "I'm doing final revisions on a children's book about a cat in a library" or "I'm working on a book review."

Nobody asks how *hard* I'm working, so I don't feel compelled to say that I've finished everything but the last sentence of the book review, or that all I'm doing for the collection of diaries and letters is looking for photographs of the people with whom my mother corresponded, or that the "final revisions" on the library cat book involve one or two word changes in a poem for very young children.

Some of this work feels like work: it might not be backbreaking labor, but it's absorbing and often delightful. Once I needed to make final revisions for the manuscript of *Homer the Library Cat* because on one page the artist had put Homer in a slightly different position than the one my words suggested. In the story, Homer travels all around town before he finally gets to the library, and at one point he visits the fire station. In the picture, the cat is reclining at his ease in a fire truck, just under the extension ladder. In the poem, however, I had Homer "behind the hook and ladder/A cozy, cat-sized space."

The original two lines made no sense anyway, my husband pointed out, because in firefighting terms, the "hook" of "hook and ladder" is really just a long pole with a hook on one end, used by firemen to pull down windows or deal with debris or perform other firefighting tasks. The hook is a tool like a fire ax rather than some generic part of a fire engine, as I had mistakenly imagined. All too often in my writing, I use a phrase—"hook and ladder" in this case—because I like the sound of it, not because I know what it means.

The editor and I deleted the word "hook" from the text and changed Homer's position from "behind the hook and ladder" to "underneath the ladder." That seemed simple enough—same rhythm, better geometry—except that I began to think that in a book for very young readers the word "underneath" is a bit of a mouthful, and the editor agreed. We changed the phrase to "Just beneath the ladder." The editor gave it some more thought, and we finally settled on "Right beneath the ladder."

That was all the revising I had to do—replacing three words with two other words—until a message came in from the British affiliate of the American publisher. More changes were needed for the British edition, to effect what is called the "Anglicization" of the book. The work required me to read the message from the British editors, look at the suggested changes, and if I agreed with these changes write "OK." These are some of the things the British editors wanted to know:

Page 9
line 1: OK to change "yarn" to "wool"?

Page 10
The word "trash" is a bit of a no-go for us Brits. The "trash cans" on page 11 are easy enough to conjure into "dustbins", but here on page 10 the rhyme makes the transformation a bit trickier. I wonder how you might feel about something along these lines:

One morning Homer heard a CRASH -
a really awful din!
He jumped out of the window
and landed in the bin.

[The original lines were:
Homer was at home alone
the day he heard a CRASH!
He jumped right out the window
and landed in the trash.]

Page 14
line 4: OK to change spelling of "cozy" to "cosy"?

Page 17
line 3: OK to change "jumped right up" to "rushed straight out"?

Page 18
line 2: OK to change "railroad" to "railway"?
line 3: OK to change "boxcar" to "goods van"?

OK, I told them. OK, OK, OK, OK, and OK. I always say OK.
Anglicization is a joy. I love "dustbins" and "goods vans" and spelling
American "z" words with a British "s." I love all this even though
the word itself, "Anglicization," sticks to my teeth when I try to pronounce it.

This all sounds like work, doesn't it? It even feels like work, because after I have spent a happy afternoon e-mailing back and forth
with my editors on all these word changes, British and American, I
think I've been very productive.

However, I sometimes feel very *un*productive. Sadly, there are
those undeniable bleak periods when I'm living in a writer's waste-
land, when an old project has been finished for some time and a new
one has not yet appeared on the horizon. If someone asks me what
I'm "working on these days," I may mumble something like, "Oh, bits
and pieces; a little of this and a little of that, you know how it is . . ."

which probably means that I've written a few grumpy pages in my journal and sent a whole bunch of e-mail messages.

I try hard to remind myself at such times that this, too, is writing, especially the pages in the journal. One year, I was writing very little for publication—or so I thought—and quite a lot in my journal. This was the period when my mother, fragile and disoriented at the end of her life, was with us on the farm. My editor called at one point and asked me his version of the question, "What are you working on these days?" I answered sadly that I wasn't working on anything, really, just writing in my journal about what it was like to have my mother with us, suffering from dementia and seeming very unlike the woman I'd known all my life. We talked for a while, then he said, "I'd like to see what you've written." After our conversation I typed out several pages from my handwritten journal and sent them to him.

That journal eventually turned into *No More Words*, a book that came directly from what I had written to help myself understand what was happening to my mother. When the book was published, I was told by a number of readers that it helped them with their own experience of caring for elderly parents. At the time I was writing in my journal that year, I was guiltily aware that I was avoiding my "real" writing. I forgot that I was avoiding it by writing.

While engaged in editing work with my mother's diaries and letters spanning 1947 to 1986, all of them written during the second half of her life but none published in her lifetime, I learned that she did the same thing I do, in her own way and to an even greater extreme. She wrote long letters to her friends and long entries in her diaries, full of apologies or self-chastisements about her inability to get enough writing done. In letter after letter, journal entry following journal entry, there are eloquent paragraphs of insight and perception and beautifully phrased sentences about her life and her relationships, prefaced by despairing comments about "not writing."

But she *was* writing. She was writing three or four letters a day as well as writing entries in her diaries about her children or her husband or difficulties in the lives of her friends. And she kept carbon copies of all this material. Now, decades later, a completed manuscript of all that she was writing has appeared in print, and the book of these writings has taken its place among her other published works.

Yet if anyone had asked her at the time what she was "working on these days," she never would have imagined this book. During those years, she was struggling with "real" books, trying to find time to get each manuscript completed while she was also living with or without her husband (depending upon his always unpredictable travel schedule), caring for her children, running her household, recording her thoughts in her journals, writing letters to friends, and worrying that she was not writing.

The title for this book of diaries and letters published after my mother's death, *Against Wind and Tide*, was chosen by her editor, and came from a phrase my mother often used to describe what it was like to try to write while raising a family and running a household. The phrase came from a letter Harriet Beecher Stowe once wrote to her sister about this same conflict in her own life:

> I am constantly pursued and haunted by the idea that I don't do anything. Since I began this note I have been called off at least a dozen times; once for the fish-man, to buy a codfish; once to see a man who had brought me some barrels of apples; once to see a book-man; then to Mrs. Upham, to see about a drawing I promised to make for her; then to nurse the baby; then into the kitchen to make a chowder for dinner; and now I am at it again, for nothing but deadly determination enables me ever to write; it is rowing against wind and tide.[10]

Because of what I have learned about my mother, when someone asks me "What are you working on these days?" I try to have faith that whatever little bits of writing I'm doing now will contribute to future work, even if I don't yet know how.

A harder question to answer is "Do you have a new book coming out?" especially if I don't. What I usually say is, "Not just yet, but someday, I hope." What I really *want* to say, in certain moods, goes into the murky realms of bitterness and self-pity: "No, I don't have a new book coming out, and I probably never will. Everybody in publishing—I mean *everybody*—hates my work, okay?" But I don't say this, because it's the kind of statement after which one is expected to rush out of the room in floods of tears, and I'm not that kind of person. So I restrain myself to, "Not just yet, but someday, I hope," and try to look cheerful and brave.

Occasionally, and happily, the answer to the book-coming-out question has been "Yes! My children's book about a cat and a library will be published in the fall," or "A collection of my mother's unpublished diaries and letters, which I helped to edit and wrote an introduction for, will be published the following spring." Phew!

There is a third question people ask me, and this is the one I really dread: "Are you still writing?" I'm never quite sure what the questioner is implying. My mind envisions a horde of unpleasant possibilities, all the things that might have been meant but were left tactfully unsaid:

Are you still writing or have you finally, thank goodness, retired?

Are you still writing, or did the surgery I heard about leave your brain impaired?

Are you still writing, even with the decline of books and newspapers?

Are you still writing, after that not-so-nice review of your last book?

Are you still writing? Shouldn't you have a blog?

They hover in the air, these possibilities, so confusing and yet so persuasive that I can't formulate an answer that makes sense. In order not to completely disgrace myself, I've learned to smile, or nod, or shrug, or all three, while remaining mute. I hope the other person will think I'm modest, as opposed to insane. After a few moments, the questioner usually wanders off, which is a relief to both of us.

Another reason the "Are you still writing?" question is so hard to answer is that to ask me "Are you still writing?" is like asking, "Are you still breathing?" Writing is the way I stay aware of being alive, the way I find out what I'm thinking, the way I understand the world. This is not only true for me, but has been true for many of my writing ancestors and near relations as well. As my mother once wrote, "In our family, an experience was not finished, not truly experienced, unless written down . . ."[11]

If I'm alive and in the room to hear the question, "Are you still writing?" I'm still writing. I like to think that I write all the time, whether I'm doing it in my head or on paper or on the computer. I like to see words and paragraphs and pages accumulate, and if I want that to happen, I have to sit down several days each week, for anything from twenty minutes to several hours a day, and put down the words. There are days when I work for one hour, days when I work for two hours, or three, or four, and days when I don't work at all. I rarely work all day long unless I have a deadline that scares me. Then I do.

I write at home, and I write in different parts of the house at different times of year. I realized this when I was asked to write a short piece about what it was like to be a writer during the winter, as opposed to other seasons of the year. My initial conclusion was that writing in winter is pretty much like writing in spring, summer, or fall, only colder. But the more I thought about it, the more I realized that this was not really true, not for me anyway.

In summer, I work upstairs in what I call my writing room, a former bedroom where the windows look out through the trees and over the fields to the far horizon. Trees and fields and far horizons are fine when the fields are green and the skies are blue and the trees wave leafy branches in the breeze. This view is uplifting. It makes me *feel* like writing . . . except when it makes me feel like taking a walk instead.

In the winter, however, I look out of my writing room windows and see bare trees and gray skies and vast stretches of sloping and unbroken whiteness. Serene, yes, and peaceful, and empty of distractions, but white fields look too much like blank pages. Not only that, but our old farmhouse heats unevenly, and when I sit upstairs for any length of time, my feet get cold.

So I come downstairs and work by the fireplace in the living room instead, with the dogs for company, and I experience the many interruptions of our winter household. I am a writer who depends upon interruption, though I've always imagined other writers, better disciplined, devoutly literary people, toiling for long hours without pause. Whether the work is going smoothly or not, whether the words are soaring or just staggering along, other writers stick at it valiantly all day long, but I don't. To do my best writing, I need to work in fairly long sessions, so that I can really sink into the words and the thoughts, but even so I write off and on during the day and during the week, and I rely on interruptions.

I can't say that interruptions make me a better writer, but I do think they keep me honest. I can't get too carried away with my thoughts or go off on too many tangents, which I tend to do, if there is a practical task to bring me back down from time to time. I work on my writing for a while, then I get up and do something else. In the summer, that could be weeding the garden or taking that walk, and it might last for an hour or more. Winter interruptions are shorter and closer to home: letting the dogs in (and then out, and then in, and then out), feeding the birds, baking bread, knitting, getting more wood from the woodshed to put on the fire. In winter, the circle around my writing is smaller, cozier, closer in, and more concentrated. My train of thought isn't so easily broken, which means that one of two things happens. I might go deeply into my thoughts and come up with profundities to share with my readers, or I might sink comfortably into my chair by the fire, fall asleep, and possibly snore a little.

Spring and fall don't last very long where I live, but they have their own interruptive opportunities. Raking leaves and planting bulbs can take me through a month of writing in October, and April is the time when our lambs are born. Most of the ewes have had some experience with giving birth and taking care of their young, but once in a while, there is a difficult birth or a young mother who rejects a newborn, and we end up with a "bottle lamb" living in a box in the kitchen, bleating loudly every few hours to be fed.

The trouble with a writing schedule that depends upon interruption is that the interruptions themselves can be so seductive. If there is a lamb, I'd really like to play with it all morning long, and then watch it sleep after the bottle-feeding. I also have to be careful about the telephone and my e-mail correspondence. Both are tantalizing, enjoyable, and self-per-petuating, but only rarely have anything to do with my work.

I can't do much to prevent lambing emergencies, but I've de-cided, regretfully, that e-mail and other online activities are forbidden to me as a writing interruption. I am allowed to look at my e-mail correspondence just before I start a writing period during the day in case something of a professional nature has been sent to me electron-ically (Anglicization!) and I can also look at e-mail after I've stopped writing for the day. I can't look at it in the middle of a writing session, because I get so distracted if I do.

I don't allow myself to answer the phone either. That's what answering machines are for, and whatever the message is, it's rarely urgent. I learned this when my children were growing up. If the phone rang, I always answered immediately, in case the call came from the school and something had happened to one of my children. Ninety-nine percent of the time, the call had nothing to do with the children or the school. The once or twice a year at most when the call was from the school, it was never an immediate emergency: one of the kids wasn't feeling well, maybe, but more often, somebody had forgotten something at home that they needed for class.

The trouble with responding to e-mail messages or answering the telephone when I'm trying to write is that I get caught up in someone else's world and lose the thread of my own thinking. I may even fall out of a writing mood that it has taken me all morning to fall *into*. Walking, gardening, knitting, baking bread, doing the laundry, and feeding lambs are all permitted. That's because these activities allow reflection and don't demand my attention in the way human conversation does, whether in person or on the telephone or online.

Conversation takes the wind right out of my writing sails and blows it away in talk. If I'm on the phone for any length of time, or if I'm engaged in an energetic exchange of e-mail messages, I know I'm not going to sit down to my writing with much appetite afterwards. It's as if I've indulged in a heavy snack too close to dinnertime and can't eat when the meal arrives.

I can understand, then, why my mother felt she was "not writing" when she filled her journals and sent off all those letters. She was exercising her writer's gifts and her writer's energy in conversation, whether with herself or with others. She wore herself out, in a sense, in conversation, and she thought this kind of communication didn't count. Of course, though, there can be treasures revealed in conversation, whether we realize it or not at the time. Words I remember and write down from a conversation that meant something to me can be just as valuable as whatever I might come up with in what I think of as my "real writing." When I was reading my mother's diaries and letters from the early 1950s, some of the insights and phrases I found there later appeared in her 1955 book, *Gift from the Sea*. Maybe, perhaps almost unconsciously, she knew she was doing her "real writing" after all.

Ideally, I think, a writing voice and a conversational voice should not be too different anyway. The writers whose work I most enjoy speak to me from the page in a very natural way, and I am happiest about my own writing when I feel as if I am talking to the person reading my words, rather than making a speech or putting on a performance. The longer I write, the more important it is to me to use my own voice and my own understandings as simply as I can. Even when I write fiction, which I don't do too often, the fictional characters are familiar to me, like relatives I might have had in another life, and the setting is a place I know or have known. If I feel acquainted with the people and the landscape, I can enter their world and imagine what happens there and write it down. For me that world will always be some form of home.

It has taken me most of my writing life to understand that my "writing place" is here where I live, and that my "writing voice" is just my regular old voice, the one I use all the time. I am aware that the most important things in my life and my work are so close to me that I didn't even fully recognize them for a long time. But all the same, the next time someone asks me, "Are you still writing?" I think I will answer, "Yes. I am."

APPENDIX

For the Lindbergh Lecture at the Smithsonian National Air and Space Museum, May 18, 2017

My parents actually did not stop flying together after the *Tingmissartoq* went to the Museum of Natural History in 1933. Just four years later, in 1937, they traveled through Asia, Africa, and Europe to study aviation conditions and air routes, but my father had ordered a new airplane for this trip, a British-built tandem-cockpit Miles Mohawk, its orange wings and black fuselage repeating the colors of the retired Lockheed Sirius.

They flew again in the Mohawk in 1938, visiting aviation factories and an air museum in Russia, and dining with aviators and Russian officials. It was that trip that marked the last long flight my parents made together in a small plane. After that flight my mother was ready to spend less of her time in the air, more of her life at home with a growing family, eventually including Jon (born in 1932), Land (1935), Anne (1940), Scott (1942), and me, Reeve, born in 1945. It was a new era in the life of the Lindberghs.

My father, however, really never did stop flying. His later experience included combat service during World War II, flying P-38s with the 475th Fighter Group in the Pacific. There he taught combat pilots how to extend the range of their missions by increasing manifold pressure and lowering revolutions per minute in their aircraft engines, reducing consumption of gasoline. He was technically a "consultant," his work related to his association with Henry Ford and the Ford Motor Company's production of military aircraft for the war. He had no military status whatsoever to protect him from the enemy had he been shot down and taken as a prisoner.

It meant a great deal to him to be able to serve his country in the war, despite—or perhaps because of—his highly controversial prewar stance against American intervention. The isolationist position was in fact shared by a large segment of the population; it was difficult for President Roosevelt to persuade the country to join the conflict until the Japanese attack on Pearl Harbor in 1941.

More than a half century following his wartime flights in the Pacific, long after his death and following my mother's passing, we found his wartime uniform—he was required to wear a Naval uniform for his missions, but one without insignia or rank—carefully folded and saved in a box that was not sent to a museum, but kept at their home through his lifetime.

After the war my father became a consultant for the Strategic Air Command, and over the following years he was engaged in a wide variety of military and scientific projects. I did not know much about his postwar work for the government, but was aware that in the 1960s he was a consultant to Pan American Airways, inspecting aircraft and flights and facilities and traveling all over the world.

He did not ever spend a lot of time at home, but when he was with us in that later period, he spoke with increasing urgency about environmental degradation worldwide, and about his fear that the very science and technology he had loved for a lifetime could be destroying the planet itself. He had come to know the earth in a way that very few other human beings ever did, flying over land and sea for more than four decades. Now he saw alarming changes taking place below his wings.

He began to travel with a new mission: to understand and preserve the uniqueness of the earth itself, its lands and waters, its natural areas, its wildlife and the traditional ways of living for human beings in the jungles of the Philippines or on the semi-arid lands of East Africa.

Never turning his back on technological progress, never ignoring the aviation and aerospace development of this era, my father was still equally at home jumping out of a helicopter onto a treetop platform in the Philippine rain forest or watching the Apollo 8 launch at Cape Kennedy. My mother traveled with him on the Apollo 8 trip in December of 1968, and also to the game parks of Africa. She was struck by the contrast of two worlds coexisting, and later wrote of lying on her back at night at a campsite near Mount Kilimanjaro with my father, looking up at the stars they had learned to know so well in aerial navigation long ago, when they suddenly saw a satellite moving in the vastness overhead.

In an essay that appeared first in *Life* magazine, then in her 1969 book, *Earth Shine*, she wrote, "In the wilderness, out of sight or hearing of other men, no light, no town, no highway visible, we were watching a man-made vehicle in space."[12] She and he were both convinced that we need both the wilderness and the satellite. As my mother, who loved birds, put it, "the heron and the astronaut are linked in an indissoluble chain of life on earth."[13]

My father wrote, even more strongly, "The human future depends on our ability to combine the knowledge of science with the wisdom of wildness."[14] If he were here speaking, that might be the phrase he would use to end his remarks tonight, but I have another one in mind, as I honor the airplanes and the people who flew them. I think in this space, we are in the realm of infinite possibility. I know that work is being done all over the world to bring together technology and nature, wisdom and wildness, even while aviation and aerospace technology continues to go forward, with developments my father would have loved, like the Air Shepherd aerial drone program that is working to combat poaching in several countries in Africa right now, or my nephew Erik Lindbergh's pioneering work with electric aircraft, promoting "quiet flight"—how my mother would love that!

Tonight, in this place that holds my parents' history, and at this moment, honoring the ninetieth anniversary of my father's 1927 flight from New York to Paris, I'd like to leave you with one of my favorite sentences from his book, *The Spirit of St. Louis*. It comes from the preface, and it applies to all the history we celebrate here tonight, and all that lies ahead.

"We actually live, today, in our dreams of yesterday; and, living in those dreams, we dream again."[15]

ACKNOWLEDGMENTS

Heartfelt and delighted thanks to the team at Brigantine Media: Neil Raphel, Janis Raye, and Adrienne Raphel, for their long friendship, steadfast encouragement, and thoughtful, thorough, and meticulous editing of this book. Thanks, too, for the unending affection and support of family members and friends, including the End of the Road Writers and the Good Living Center memoir writing group. I am deeply grateful to you all.

NOTES

1. Charles A. Lindbergh, *We* (New York: G. P Putnam, 1927), 23.

2. Brendan Gill, *Lindbergh Alone* (New York: Harcourt Brace Jovanovich, 1977), 67.

3. Charles A. Lindbergh, *The Spirit of St. Louis* (New York: Charles Scribner's Sons, 1953), 247.

4. Peg Bracken, *The I Hate to Housekeep Book* (New York: Harcourt, Brace, & World, 1962).

5. Mae Savell Croy, *Putnams' Household Handbook* (New York: G. P. Putnam's Sons, 1916), 71.

6. Anne Morrow Lindbergh, *Against Wind and Tide*, ed. Reeve Lindbergh (New York: Random House, 2012), 27.

7. Tom McNamee, "Rognons de Veau à la Moutarde," *Tomfoodery* (April 9, 2012). http://info.tomfoodery.net/2012/04/rognons-de-veau-la-moutarde.html

8. A. Scott Berg, *Lindbergh* (New York: G. P. Putnam's Sons, 1998), 291.

9. Anne Morrow Lindbergh, *North to the Orient* (Orlando: Harvest/Harcourt, Inc., 1967) 59.

10. Harriet Beecher Stowe and Charles Edward Stowe, *Life of Harriet Beecher Stowe, Compiled from Her Letters and Journals by Her Son, Charles Edward Stowe* (Andesite Press, 2015).

11. Anne Morrow Lindbergh, *Bring Me a Unicorn* (San Diego: Harvest/Harcourt, Inc., 1971), xvi.

12. Anne Morrow Lindbergh, *Earth Shine* (New York: Harcourt, Brace & World, 1969), xi.

13. Anne Morrow Lindbergh, "The Heron and the Astronaut," *Life* 66, no. 8 (February 28, 1969): 26.

14. Charles A. Lindbergh, "The Wisdom of Wildness," *Life* 63, no. 25 (December 22, 1967): 10.

15. Lindbergh, *The Spirit of St. Louis*, xi.

Made in the USA
Middletown, DE
16 February 2019